LAND
T

THE SOUTH WEST OF ENGLAND

Edited by Lorraine Weeks & Graham Blight

FRANCES LINCOLN LIMITED
PUBLISHERS

Acknowledgements

Introduction by Archie Miles

Site entries written by Sheila Ashton

Researched by Lorraine Weeks, Helen Parr, Tina Newton & Lesley Silvera

Edited by Lorraine Weeks & Graham Blight

Maps by Linda M Dawes, Belvoir Cartographics & Design

Photographic acknowledgements

Adrian Colston: 81, 82, Bob Corns, English Nature: 108,
Cornwall Wildlife Trust: 45, Helen Parr: 17, 27, 35, 39, 74, 76, 79, 80, 84, 85, 88,
Lesley Silvera: 1, 12, 53, 55, 56, 57, 59, 61, 66, 67, Lorraine Weeks: 26, 31, 34, 103,
National Trust: 2 (Magnus Rew), 11 (Stephen Robson), 28 (Dennis G. Madge), 33
(Brian Muelnner), 37 (G. Taylor), 43 (G. Taylor), 47, 50, 51 (Andrew Besley), 54
(Peter Cade), 70, 71, 72 (Magnus Rew), 99 (Martin Piper), 113
Woodland Trust: 21, 38, 40, 75, 86, 89, 95 (Mike Brown), 110, 117, 118, 123

Frances Lincoln Ltd
4 Torriano Mews
Torriano Avenue
London NW5 2RZ
www.franceslincoln.com

The South West of England
Copyright © Frances Lincoln 2006
Text © Woodland Trust 2006

First Frances Lincoln edition: 2006

A catalogue record for this book is available
from the British Library.

ISBN 10: 0-7112-2602-4
ISBN 13: 978-0-7112-2602-9

Printed and bound in Singapore
The paper used in this book was sourced from
sustainable forests, managed according to FSC
(Forest Stewardship Council) guidelines.

1 2 3 4 5 6 7 8 9

Half title page Hawkcombe

Title page Teign Valley

Contents

o

How to use this guide

Covering a region that encompasses the Southwest: Cornwall, Devon, Somerset, Dorset, Wiltshire and the Bristol area, this book is divided into three areas represented by key maps on pp18-19, 48-49 and 90-91. The tree symbols on these maps denote the location of each wood. In the pages following the key maps, the sites nearest one another are described together (wherever practical) to make planning a day out as rewarding as possible.

For each site entry the name of the nearest town/village is given, followed by road directions and the grid reference of the site entrance. The area of the site (in hectares followed by acres) is given together with the official status of the site where appropriate and the owner, body or organisation responsible for maintaining the site. Symbols are used to denote information about the site and its facilities as explained in the next column.

Symbols used denote information about each site and the facilities to be found there.

Type of wood

Mainly broadleaved woodland
Mainly coniferous woodland
Mixed woodland

Car park

Parking on site   P
Parking nearby   P
Parking difficult to find

Official status

Area of Outstanding Natural Beauty
AONB
Site of Special Scientific Interest   SSSI

Site facilities

Sign at entry
Information board
One or more paths suitable for
  wheelchair users
Dogs allowed under supervision
Waymarked trail
Toilet
Picnic area
Entrance/car park charge   £
Refreshments on site

The South West of England

Savernake Forest

Dappled sunlight plays games of kiss–chase as it flirts with one elephant-grey beech bole after another. Limpid emerald swathes of brand-new beech leaves suffuse the woodland floor with their green glow. Before the beech came full-flush wood anemones, and bluebells did their annual best, but once the massive old beeches mellow and darken, plant life on the woodland floor will have to scrap a little harder for its day in the sun.

   No matter, whatever the time of year, Savernake Forest, just to the south of the lucky community of Marlborough, provides a splendid woodland experience. Strangely enough the name Savernake means 'Severn oak', which may derive from a common river name, but equally from severed (i.e. cut, coppiced or pollarded) oak. Oaks are here, but first impressions are of a beech-dominant woodland, and there are some beauties – massive old multi-stemmed maidens and outgrown pollards are everywhere, and all along the three or four miles of the poker-straight Grand Avenue tall beeches line the way. Explore any of the numerous rides and paths and you soon find some of the craggy old oaks lurking in the forest depths. Some are dead, many are dying, it's the natural law after all, but in their dotage they stand as great green monuments. On the western edge of the forest, hanging precariously over the A346, stands the resolute form of the Big Belly Oak (once also known as the Decanter Oak). With a girth of 36 feet, it is thought to be in excess of 1000 years old, and local legend has it that dancing naked, 12 times anti-clockwise around the tree at midnight will make the Devil appear.

Savernake is at the centre of one of Wiltshire's larger concentrations of woodland. A glance at the central area of the county, devoted largely to Salisbury Plain, or even the chalky Downs between Swindon and Marlborough cannot open up many substantial woodland offerings, but at the northern end of the county one of Britain's 12 Community Forests, which came into being back in 1994, is doing its level best to redress the balance. The Great Western Community Forest aims to provide more and better access to woodlands around Swindon – an area of some 168 square miles. Ultimately this will improve the environment in which people live, diversify land use, revitalise derelict land and enhance the local biodiversity. The results are more pleasant, healthier, greener environments for leisure, recreation, education and social and economic development.

Wiltshire is also blessed with many small individual woodland sites which are well worth seeking out. Blackmoor Copse is one of Wiltshire Wildlife Trust's excellent locations, and is to be found about six miles east of Salisbury. In particular this wood is noted for its dormice, shy little creatures and not easily found, but you will be entranced if you do, and 30 of Britain's 55 native butterfly species have been recorded here. One particular rarity is the delicate pearl-bordered fritillary, a species whose caterpillars rely on the leaves of violets as their food plant. Regular coppicing at Blackmoor has created small clearings in the wood where these delicate little plants can thrive and also nourish the butterflies. A couple of mysteries attend this wood. Who planted the magnificent row of yews? Was this an old boundary? And why is the body of water at the eastern edge of the reserve called King Charles' Pond? In the greater scheme of things it doesn't really matter, but for visitors there is a chance here to go pond dipping and, if you're lucky, you'll find a great crested newt in your net. This spectacular little amphibian is our rarest newt and is most readily identified by the bright orange belly with black spots. There is something wonderfully primeval about these little beasts – a prehistoric monster in miniature. Please be careful to put everyone back in their pond home though.

Before leaving Wiltshire mention must be made of a truly inspiring collection of trees and woodland at the National Trust's Stourhead. Go in autumn, on a still day, when the colours are breathtaking, and the wonderful mirrored glory across the lake is awesome.

Neighbouring Somerset has, in some ways, a similar pattern of woodland distribution to Wiltshire, namely that the central part of the county, dominated by The Levels, is largely devoid of woodland. To the east around the limestone hills and gorges of the Mendips lie some fascinating woods, often containing the rarer native trees such as whitebeams and limes, but usually dominated by ash and hazel.

Long Wood, near Cheddar, and Ebbor Gorge just north of Wells, make an excellent introduction to these woodland types. The flora is rich, particularly in spring, with a succession of wood anemones, primroses, bluebells and the distinctive reek of wild garlic. In the wetter areas these woods are host to a wealth of mosses and ferns, and it's worth coming prepared with some sturdy boots as the rugged limestone and steep paths can be pretty challenging. Something else that unites all these woods is the remarkable views out across The Levels. Be up on the tops on a spring or autumn morning when the mists are starting to rise and watch the landscape slowly revealing its trees, hedgerows and habitations to a new day.

Head westward, and the woods of the Quantocks are reached. Both Great Wood and Hawkridge are mixtures of native broadleaves and conifers. Hawkridge contains an old lime kiln and remains of old quarries, yet another indication that woodlands and industry were once mutual companions, and if you're lucky you may spot both red and roe deer here. Explore the numerous paths of Great Wood and enjoy the splendour of massive Douglas firs or feathery larch plantations – emerald green in spring with their tiny

Stourhead

pink larch 'rose' flowers or golden hued in autumn. Sparrow hawks, redstarts, pied flycatchers and wood warblers all make their homes in this wood, and at dusk you might catch a badger shuffling across your path. At the western limits of Somerset lies the wild and rugged expanse of Exmoor. In itself it is not a particularly well-wooded area, seemingly belying its name of Exmoor Forest. However, forest it is, more by ancient hunting jurisdiction than the popular perception of a wooded habitat; and yet some of the valleys which run off Exmoor contain some startlingly beautiful woods, and none better than Horner Wood. Owned by the National Trust since 1918, this upland hazel and sessile oak wood is one of the largest single areas of ancient semi-natural woodland in southern England, and designated as a National Nature Reserve. Historically, the regime in this wood was of coppicing, both for charcoal and tan bark, and there is evidence of this in the remains of old charcoal

Horner Wood

hearths and an iron-smelting site. Today management here is a mixture of coppicing, most particularly for wildlife benefit, but also with areas of non intervention, and there is wildlife aplenty here. The wood is most remarkable for its many bat species, around 240 different lichens, and in the autumn a fungus foray could turn up more than 400 different species.

Near the chocolate-box-quaint village of Shaftesbury, in Dorset, Duncliffe Wood cloaks the twin-topped saddle of Duncliffe Hill in the Vale of Blackmore. Local legend has it that this wood inspired Thomas Hardy to write his novel The Woodlanders, and a walk here reaffirms the inspirational nature of the place. In spring the carpets of bluebells, particularly in some of the ash-dominated compartments, where the early sunlight floods the ground unhindered, are unparallelled in their blue-sea splendour and the intoxication of their smell. This is a wood steeped in history and probably containing some of the oldest trees in the whole of Dorset; try and find them – not the huge old boles you might expect, but giant multi-stemmed coppice stools of small-leaved limes, cut in a regular regime for maybe 1000 years. This has been the mechanism of their survival. An ancient track known as Hort's Way passes through the wood and there is much evidence of old earth-bank boundaries here too. The Woodland Trust bought this wood from the Forestry Commission in 1984 and has subsequently been working to restore the natural broadleaf cover in the parts that were coniferised. You can find numerous plants which indicate the ancient origins of this wood and many butterflies which are attracted to the clearings and rides which have been created, including rarities such as white admiral, purple hairstreak and silver-washed fritillary.

Woodland means different things to different people. There is little doubt that most of us find time to slow down, draw refreshment for the soul, put the hurly-burly of our frantic existence on the back burner, and simply soak up the glories that nature has to offer when we visit a wood. However, our children haven't reached the point in their lives where this is so imperative. The wonder of wildlife is one thing, but woods with plenty of potential for activities are what they also need, and Moors Valley Forest & Country Park fits the bill handsomely. This is essentially a vast conifer plantation, just east of the New Forest on the Hampshire/Dorset border, where you can really go for it! Hire bikes, climb ropes, enjoy wooden play structures or get up in the tree-top trail and enjoy a whole new perspective of the woods. When you're exhausted the kids will drag you into the shop to buy goodies or you can collapse in the tearoom with a well-earned cuppa. Incidentally, nature hasn't been sidelined here, as the ranger team runs an events programme and frequently offers guided walks; and if you can calm down long enough you could spot nightjars, goldcrests, roe deer and sand lizards here too.

Before moving west out of Dorset mention must be made of the remarkable and unusual events down on the coast. In 1839 the Dowlands Landslip near Lyme Regis opened up a huge chasm beneath the chalk cliffs, which has subsequently grown up into what might legitimately be described as primary woodland – i.e. natural colonisation of virgin ground. Ash is the dominant species here – little surprise there then – but there is a splendid array of plants, including madder and stinking iris, and hart's tongue fern in abundance. A cracking walk along the coast with beautiful views.

The coastline around Britain presents us with an infinite variety of woodland, and much of it containing extremely rare plants which, due to the nature of the precipitous terrain, have remained naturally protected. The cliff-top woods of North Devon contain some remarkable plants and trees. For example, Keivill's Wood, which is part of the Woodland Trust's Buck's Valley Woods, is host to the rare Devon whitebeam, most easily spotted in the springtime with its creamy pale green leaves emerging, and later on with clusters of dank-smelling cream flowers.

Farther west, along the coast, exploring the Heddon Valley makes a good day's trip. The options here are to walk, ride or cycle, and either way to appreciate the very best the North Devon landscape has to offer. Typically the woods are principally Devon stalwart oak, much of which hangs doggedly to the steep and craggy slopes, but the paths and bridleways here also weave through ash, hazel and beech, and of course, that universal interloper, sycamore. There are glorious hedgebanks here too, adorned with wild strawberry, red campion, herb robert, foxgloves, the distinctive fleshy little green button leaves of pennywort and everywhere the hart's tongue fern. Another bonus feature of coastline woods is the wonderful mixture of birdlife. At one turn pied flycatchers and wood warblers; at another razorbills and guillemots.

Established in 1998, to give the West Country's woodlands a huge boost, the South West Forest, an independent non-commercial partnership, is providing training, advice, funding, information networking and general encouragement to the communities and landowners of the Dartmoor, Exmoor and Bodmin Moor regions, with the aim of increasing tree cover from 10% to 15%. This task will mean the planting of some 15,000 hectares of trees over the next 15 years, and many diverse planting types will be undertaken, including commercial farm woodland, mixed woodland and copses, community woods, orchards, hedgerow trees and domestic sites. The intention is to improve the environment, both for wildlife biodiversity and landscape conservation, as well as creating more amenity sites for the local populace and the tourism influx. There should also be a marked improvement in the rural economy, particularly in the farming fraternity, whose livelihoods have become increasingly precarious in recent years.

Across Dartmoor the vista is wild and barren and few trees make it their business to even try to survive the rigours of this challenging terrain, and yet the valleys, which run off the moor contain some luxuriant and extremely picturesque woodland. A glance at the map reveals numerous woodland enclaves playing perfect accompaniment to the river valley system.

For that feeling of liberation so often generated by vast wide-open spaces you could do worse than try the expansive landscapes of Fernworthy Forest. Get a lungful of moorland air, laced with reservoir, forest and great views all in one burst. A stark contrast to this largely 20th-century manmade forest of conifers are the ancient, but also manmade, stone circles and stone rows of the Bronze Age.

Along the river Dart lies Holne Wood, one of Dartmoor's largest stretches of native oak woodland. Oakwood it may be, but there are also some fine beeches here too. High-level paths take you along the valley top to soak up the stunning views. Low-level paths follow the Dart as it tumbles deep through the valley bottom. When it's quiet keep a weather eye open for otters here. When the river's crashing furiously after swelling storm waters, marvel as expert canoeists tackle the white-water rapids.

Once off the moors many will be drawn to the sandy seashore of resorts such as Torquay and Paignton, but even here there are opportunities to quit the deck chair, pack a picnic and sidle off to enjoy the woodland delights of the coast. The Marridge, Elberry and Grove Wood group is perched high on a headland with glorious sea views all around. Although containing planted larch and sweet chestnut, The Grove is essentially an ancient semi-natural woodland, containing ash, beech and oak, as well as rare whitebeams and an understorey with the spiky butcher's broom and the often overlooked spindle, which only gives its exotic show in autumn with bright-pink fruits, which split to reveal vivid orange interiors. Beneath the woods are seven old limestone quarries and remains of limekilns. However, on a hot summer's day the treat in store is to end up in Elberry Cove with your toes tickled by the briny.

Cross the Tamar into Cornwall and immediately make a detour to enjoy the Cotehele Estate. A leisurely boat trip along the river makes an excellent introduction to the valley and its woodland, but once ashore there's plenty of exploration potential to keep everyone happy. The woods vary in composition from sessile oak and ash through to beech, sweet chestnut and conifers and are renowned for their birdlife; sparrow hawks, barn owls, lesser-spotted woodpeckers, garden warblers and wood warblers having all been found here. There's also the old quay to visit, a working water mill, museum, the Chapel in the Wood and of course the splendid National Trust property of Cotehele House and its beautiful gardens.

For something rather more rugged, a visit to the Golitha Falls National Nature Reserve, on the southern edge of Bodmin Moor, is a must. Records reveal that coppice management of this wood goes back to the time of the Domesday Book, but the regime now is largely one of non-intervention. Wild and dramatic is truly the perfect description here, as the river Fowey tumbles and splashes its way through a wet world dripping with mosses and lichens. Although oak and ash hold sway on the steep sides of the gorge there is also a fine old planted beech avenue, again notable for the lichens festooning the upper branches. Any time of year is great at Golitha, but stepping out on a bright winter's day after heavy rainstorms will be particularly rewarding.

Life for trees in the salt-laden air of Cornwall is tough, and many species simply can't cope with it. Oak is king here, but seldom in the form of large trees. As in Devon, but here even more so, small and previously coppiced trees line the steep river valleys. The wetter flushes will support alder while the drier rockier ground is often covered in a dense understorey of holly. Perhaps the most

Cotehele

remarkable woods of Cornwall are those which line the Fowey, Fal
and Helford river estuaries. Many of these woods are private and
inaccessible, but a taster may be had at Ethy on the upper reaches
of the river Fowey. There is mixed woodland here, including the
uncommon wild service tree, and yet again plenty of oaks, but most
remarkably this woodland has its roots tucked well into the muddy
shoreline of the salty river Lerryn and seems perfectly happy.

   This book will point you to an amazing array of different
woodlands with lots of diverse natural history and a good measure
of social and industrial history into the bargain. There are woods off
the beaten track, parkland and estate woods of the great old West
Country houses, lots of coastal woods with great views, as well as
the country park sites with lots of amenities and space to let loose.
That's the beauty of woods – there's something to suit everyone. So,
get your boots on and get out there!

ARCHIE MILES

MAP 1

Northam

Bideford

Clovelly
Wood

Buck's
Valley
Woods

A39

A388

Knott's &
Parsonage
Woods

A3124

South
Molton

A361

A377

Stratton
A3072

Bude

A388

Holsworthy

A386

A3072

Crediton

A3072

Cookworthy
Forest

A3079

Okehampton

Exeter

Launceston
A395

melford

A30

Lydford
Forest

MAP 2 (see p48)

A386

Moretonhampstead

A382

A38

Bodmin
Moor

A388

Greenscombe
Wood

Dartmoor

A380

lla &
rice
ods

Cadsonbury
Wood

Callington

Tavistock

Newton
Abbot

A379

38

Golitha
Falls

A390

Cotehele
Estate

A386

Buckfastleigh

Paignton

iel

Liskeard

Warleigh Point

A385

Totnes

Deerpark
Forest

Saltash

A387

Mount

Plymouth

A38

A3122

thy
ood

Looe

Edgcumbe
Country
Park

Ivybridge

Dartmouth

A379

A381

Kilminorth
Wood

A379

Kingsbridge

Salcombe

19

MAP 1

Buck's Valley Woods
Buck's Mill

Head east from Clovelly on A39. Turn left at Buck's Cross and follow road around to right, down hill past church. At bottom of hill, before village, turn right into public car park. Information board and entrance to woods off car park.

(SS352235), 41ha (102acres), SSSI, AONB

Woodland Trust

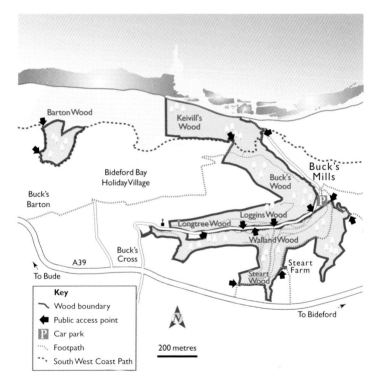

Lying on the steep valley sides and cliffs of North Devon's wooded coastal fringe, Buck's Valley Woods boast three major draws for visitors.

They are important from a conservation point of view, sustaining a host of nationally important species; they offer spectacular views of the countryside and sea; and Keivill's Wood, the key site of the group, stands on its own merit as an important sessile oak woodland.

The woods are made up of Barton, Buck's, Keivill's, Steart's, Loggins and Walland woods and enclose the tiny village of Buck's Mill east of Clovelly.

Strings of sausage and lungworm lichens – nationally rare species – grow in Keivill's Wood, a designated site of special scientific interest, along with Devon whitebeam. The surrounding woods provide a buffer zone and are important as a habitat for migrating species. All can be explored via the North Devon coastal path and other public footpaths running through and linking them, which active visitors could use to create a circular route.

Wood rush, bilberry, ferns and bluebells can be enjoyed here though some areas have become colonised with rhododendron and laurel. Work is in hand to control these.

Most of the woodland is dry and well drained but down in the valley bottoms, near to the streams and spring heads, the ground is wet year-round.

Buck's Valley Woods

MAP 1

Clovelly Wood
Bideford

Take A39 to Clovelly Cross, then B3237 down hill for 2.5km (1.5 miles). Follow 'All vehicles for Clovelly' sign to main Visitor Centre car park (SS315245), 200ha (494acres), SSSI

The Clovelly Estate Co Ltd

Clovelly Woods are a nationally important habitat for lichens with more than 250 different species, including two sub-tropical varieties unique in the UK.

The privately owned site is full of birdsong with blue tits and chaffinches flitting through the oak canopy. Look out for Devon whitebeam, and veteran trees in the parkland visible from the coast path, carpets of bluebells in May and bladder campion on the cliff.

The Hobby Drive passes through 3.5 miles of the woodland. Built in the early 19th century, it follows the contour of the land crossing four streams round deeply incised valleys before affording roof top views of the pretty fishing village of Clovelly and across the Bristol Channel.

The estate owners levy a charge for car parking and entry to the wood but walkers following the south west coast path can wander through this semi-natural woodland as part of the long distance route.

The owners have provided a visitor centre, complete with mini-shopping centre, just north of the section known as Hobby Woods.

Knott's and Parsonage Woods
Newton St Petrock

Travel southwest along A388 from Bideford, take sign on right for Newtown St Petrock, drive into village and park beside church. Walk down road leading south from church past the farm on right. Keep on road as it turns right. First farm gate on left gives access to a cart track which stops after 260m at the boundary of two fields. Follow field boundary for 160m to Knotts Wood and along side of wood to entrance gate.
(SS407112), 13ha (32acres)

Mrs J Wolfe

70-foot-high coppiced oaks, festooned with ivy help create a tropical rainforest effect – just one of the attractions of delightful Knott's and Parsonage Woods.

Knott's Wood is an ancient semi-natural woodland which includes a derelict old farm and features a wet area, where alder and goat willow were once coppiced, along with two hayfields.

The woods feature lovely old oak, beech and holly along with a pretty central meadow area teeming with black knapweed, hawkweed, yarrow and tormentil.

This is a pretty and well-loved wood though getting in and around can be a challenge. Access is via a wooden railway-sleeper bridge which becomes slippery in the wet. There are few worn paths to guide the visitor through the wood, instead walkers make use of tracks left by tractors carrying out thinning work on the site.

MAP 1

Cookworthy Forest
Holsworthy

The forest car park is just north of Halwill Junction on the A3079 Okehampton-Holsworthy road. On the opposite side of the road is Cookworthy Forest Centre. (SS413013), 850ha (2101acres)

Forestry Commission

Those seeking to get away from it all in the peace and quiet of the countryside can find a woodland haven within Cookworthy Forest, thanks to its enormous size.

This rich mix of plantation woodland offers plenty of opportunity to escape the crowds and get back to nature to enjoy the sights and sounds of a wood that's alive with wildlife.

Resident are red deer, badgers, dormice, otters and bats, all of which enjoy the forest habitat along with buzzards, ravens, wood warblers, nightjars and owls.

A network of forest tracks and paths, including a 2.6km waymarked walk, weave around the mix of oak, ash, willow, rowan and Sitka spruce that make up the wood.

It's a dynamic mixture in terms of age too, with ongoing programmes of timber felling and new planting. A variety of butterflies frequent the sunny open areas created by the felling.

Lydford Forest
Lydford

Heading south on the A30 from Okehampton join the A386 at Sourton Down. Turn right off the A386 into Lydford village. In the centre of the village turn right at the war memorial and continue along this road for approximately 1km (0.5 mile) before turning left on to the signposted forest track. (SX495850), 154ha (381acres)

Forestry Commission

This lovely wooded valley on Dartmoor's edge provides some fantastic views down the River Lyd and across towards the hills.

The woodland is a mix of broadleaf and conifer with large Douglas fir and areas of western oak. As you venture in via the well-maintained, sometimes steep forest tracks, you can appreciate the peace and quiet that encourages a wide variety of wildlife.

Red and roe deer, badgers, otters and dormice are all here, along with dipper, kingfisher, buzzard and raven.

Part of the forest is a butterfly conservation reserve. Here the heath fritillary can be seen among an array of butterflies including small pearl-bordered fritillary, dark green fritillary and grizzled skipper.

Extra points of interest to look out for are the archaeological features such as an ancient Bronze Age hill fort, listed as a scheduled ancient monument, and the many leats (drainage channels) leading to the tin-mining areas adjacent to the river Lyd.

Greenscombe Wood
Callington / Gunnislake
From Callington take the A390 towards Gunnislake. Follow signs from this road to Luckett. Having descended into Luckett village, take first lane on right and park in village car park. Continue on foot along lane to enter wood. (SX391733), 50ha (124acres), SSSI, AONB
Duchy of Cornwall

Birdsong and the sound of the river make pleasant travelling companions through this peaceful wood, set on the banks of the River Tamar.

A level main track through the wood follows the route of the 30-mile Tamar Valley discovery trail,

which forms the historic boundary between Devon and Cornwall.

Set in open countryside, the woodland mix of conifers and broadleaves, including sessile oak, provides a contrast of species and a variety of habitats.

Much of the site is a designated site of special scientific interest, thanks to the range of butterfly species. The nationally endangered heath fritillary spends summer days in the rides, grassland and clearings, where lesser butterfly orchid and common twayblade grow.

Insect-attracting plants include guelder rose and honeysuckle. A variety of ferns thrive among the ground flora, including the nationally rare bladder seed and bastard balm.

MAP 1

Golitha Falls
Liskeard

From A38 Bodmin to Liskeard road, heading east, take minor road off to left at Doublebois heading north signed Minions/Redgate. Follow this road for 5.6km (3 miles), until signs for Golitha Falls on left. Or from A30 (westbound) leave trunk road at Bolventor/Jamaica Inn turning. Golitha Falls are signed from Bolventor along minor road heading south.
(SX220687), 18ha (44acres), SSSI
English Nature

Picturesque, dripping with mosses and lichens and with the raging River Fowey flowing through in spectacular cascades, this ancient woodland is wet – and a little wild.

This verdant reserve stands on a steep-sided valley gorge with lots of ancient semi-natural sessile oak, ash and beech regeneration amid woodrush and bramble which, on a sunny day, are bathed in dappled green light.

This wood has been coppiced since the days of the Domesday Book while management today is largely non-interventional, although some coppicing is still done.

Golitha Falls

Cadsonbury Woods

Cadsonbury Wood
Callington

From Callington take the A390 west towards Liskeard. Cross the River Lynher at Newbridge, and immediately turn left down a narrow road. Car park on left. (SX347679), 10ha (24acres)

National Trust

History is just a short walk away on a visit to Cadsonbury Wood, which lines the banks of the meandering River Lynher.

The area is dominated by the Iron Age hill fort of Cadsonbury, with its large rampart and ditch, which boasts excellent views of the woods below and surrounding countryside – vital for the defence of the fort during its occupation. And within the woodland itself you can find the remains of old tin workings, where surface deposits were excavated, rather than deep mines.

History aside, this lovely oak woodland offers a choice of delightful walks. There are three colour-coded circular trails ranging from a short stroll, suitable for wheelchair and pushchair access, to a more adventurous route taking in a strenuous climb through gorse and bracken up to the hill fort.

27

MAP 1

Cotehele Estate
Callington

After crossing the Tamar bridge into Cornwall on the A38, turn right at first roundabout towards Callington on the A388. After St Mellion turn right at roundabout and follow brown signs to Cotehele. Park at Cotehele Quay.
(SX424682), 65ha (160acres), AONB
National Trust

For a not-to-be-missed treat, take a day out exploring the Cotehele Estate in the Tamar Valley.

There is so much to see and enjoy, including a visit to the quay, a working water mill, museum, the Chapel in the Wood, Cotehele House and its gardens. In summer it is sometimes possible to take a boat trip along the River Tamar.

Popular in high season, it is still easy to escape the crowds by venturing into the wooded areas away from the quay. Rising steeply up from the mud flats of the Tamar, they vary from sessile oak and ash to beech and sweet chestnut and conifer plantations. Some bear evidence of a once busy copper-mining industry,

Walking conditions vary from level, wide paths to narrow, steep ways. En route, you might glimpse some fine views of the river with Devon beyond on the opposite bank.

Cotehele Estate

Warleigh Point
Plymouth

From the A38 head towards Tavistock on the A386, take the B3373 to Tamerton Foliot. In Tamerton Foliot take 3rd left after the church into Station Road and follow the tidal creek until you reach the end of the road. (SX450608), 30ha (74acres), AONB

Devon Wildlife Trust

Set in the Tamar Valley Area of Outstanding Natural Beauty, Warleigh Point is a fine example of Devon coastal ancient oak woodland.

The wood comes alive with colour in spring when bluebells, primroses and ransoms (wild garlic) bloom alongside sweet woodruff, wood anemone and the unusual butchers broom.

This richly diverse wood boasts ancient sessile oaks, with sweet chestnut, birch, wild service, hazel, guelder rose, alder, buckthorn and spindle adding to the abundant mix.

Woodpeckers and owls make homes in the trees and coppiced areas provide open glades and scrub attracting butterflies, crickets and birds.

A good level path, accessible to wheelchairs via a special gate, leads along a route dotted with log seats to Warleigh Point. This is a great picnic spot with wonderful views of the wide Tamar estuary – a haven for redshank, golden eye and egret – and the impressive Tamar bridge beyond.

MAP 1

Mount Edgcumbe Country Park
Plymouth

From the A38 follow signs for Mount Edgcumbe on the A374 and B3247 until you reach a sign for Barrow car park or from the Torpoint car ferry follow signs for Mount Egdcumbe to the B3247, heading east until you reach a sign for Barrow car park. The Cremyll foot ferry from Plymouth brings you directly to Mount Edgcumbe's entrance.
(SX448527), 40ha, (99acres)
Cornwall County Council & Plymouth City Council

A coastal location, multitude of activities and fascinating landscaping, Mount Edgcumbe Country Park has all the makings of a great family day out.

The centrepiece of the estate is a 1550s house built by Sir Richard Edgcumbe of Cotehele and nearby is Earl's Garden, which features a number of ancient and rare specimen trees, including a 400-year-old lime, with a total of 180 different species.

Britain's largest cork oak tree is sited near the house – it was grafted onto a turkey oak in 1762.

There are other areas of woodland with formal and majestic old trees dating back 200 years. Stone structures and benches dotted around the site hint at how the woods would have looked in their 18th century heyday.

The coastal path runs through the woods where beech, oak and sweet chestnut stand alongside Cypress fir, palms and other exotics and spring brings a show of bluebells.

Cardinham Woods
Bodmin

Exit the A30 at Bodmin (ignore signs to Cardinham) and join the A38 towards Liskeard. Follow brown tourist signs to Cardinham Woods.
(SX100667), 265ha, (655acres)
Forestry Commission

Cardinham Woods has a feeling of safety and security while enjoying a sense of excitement and discovery wondering what's around the corner.

Accessible and well signed, it boasts a variety of forest types, mainly conifers and some broadleaves, set on a hillside where you can wander up long tracks

Cardinham Woods

beneath huge, majestic, moss-clad conifers in varying hues of green. One particular area, with stunningly graceful conifers, is a real treat.

Looking down across the forest's slopes, conifers merge into oaks and mature woodland of holly, oak, beech and hazel as you listen to a bubbling brook rushing down from Bodmin Moor.

Four well-thought-out routes provide a variety of challenges from easy to strenuous. As you ascend through the forest you move from high conifer forest to open felled areas, with views of Cardinham Valley and glimpses of Bodmin.

MAP 1

Lanhydrock
Bodmin

Just off the A30 south of Bodmin, follow brown tourist sign from roundabout on B3268. Best access to woods via Respryn car park, reached by taking first left after coming off the A38. Car park on left just before Fowey River.
(SX088642), 162ha (400acres)
National Trust

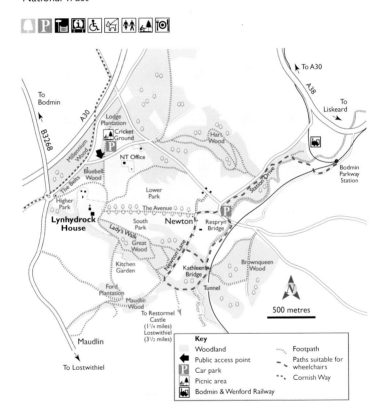

Key

⬛ Woodland	⋯ Footpath
◀ Public access point	– – Paths suitable for wheelchairs
🅿 Car park	
🅰 Picnic area	•• Cornish Way
🚂 Bodmin & Wenford Railway	

Lanhydrock

Treat yourself – and take an entire day to soak up the atmosphere of this beautiful site.

Stunning, sweeping views of a big, grand and wide-open landscape, surrounded by woodlands, greet the visitor to this 'must see' area, which has so much to absorb.

There is a great deal to take in, from veteran trees to a magnificent avenue of beech and sycamore framing the approach to the house. Then there's the Ha Ha, Victorian walled gardens, riverside walk and a plantation with giant redwood and remnants of corn mills. The Brown Queen Wood is where oak was stripped for the tanning industry.

Lanhydrock's ancient trees are home to 100 different species of lichen, not to mention mosses, bats, beetles and birds – among them tree creeper, tawny owl, nuthatch and three types of woodpecker.

There are plenty of walks, of varying lengths, including a wheelchair-accessible route and a track through 'Great Wood' – an interesting mix including yew, beech, Scots pine and even bamboo – famed for its brilliant spring carpet of bluebells. This wood has the feel of a site that, while ancient, was well used for woodland walks by the former owners of the house. And the further away from the house, the more natural and undisturbed the character of the wood becomes.

Three planted Plymouth pears – found naturally on only two sites in Devon and Cornwall and a part of English Nature's species recovery programme – can be found near Lady's Walk.

MAP 1

Cabilla and Redrice Woods
Bodmin

From the A38, 5km (3 miles) east of Bodmin, take the turning towards Cardinham. Cross bridge over the River Fowey, and take first track on right. Park in layby on right. Follow public footpath signs past sawmill (marked on map as Cabilla Farm). Reserve entrance just beyond sawmill.
(SX129652), 77ha (189acres)
Cornwall Wildlife Trust

The character of Cabilla and Redrice Woods was shaped by the once-raging appetite of Cornwall's tin industry.

It's an interesting and diverse site with a variety of habitats. Wood pasture clothing the valley bottom has an open feeling with a diverse floral range.

Much of this semi-natural woodland was coppiced for charcoal making and a couple of times Redrice was felled completely. Evidence is dotted throughout in the form of adits, the larger underground passage of which is now an important site for the rare greater and lesser horseshoe bats.

Today Redrice is a stronghold of the blue ground beetle, its floor is carpeted with ferns, and trees are festooned with mosses and lichens.

The pied flycatcher can be heard in spring, while a woodland pond is home to insects, frogs, toads and palmate newts. The track, wet in winter, is quite hard going so not the place for an easy woodland stroll.

Cabilla and Redrice Woods

Deerpark Forest
Liskeard

Just west of Liskeard turn off the
A390 at East Taphouse onto the
B3359 towards Looe. After 4km
(2.5 miles) turn left towards
Herodsfoot. After 1km (0.5km)
turn right into Deerpark Forest
car park.
(SX196605), 300ha (741acres)
Forestry Commission

Deerpark Forest

This large complex of Cornish
woodland is a haven for wildlife,
including deer, and buzzards can
be often heard, circling above
the trees.

The site is a managed forest set
on the sloping upper reaches of
the West Looe river and is made
up of a variety of mixed conifer
plantations interspersed with
broadleaves. Among these you will
find oak, beech, birch, hazel
coppice, ash and willow, with
bracken growing beneath.

It's a great site for leisurely walks
and an excellent network of forest
tracks and paths allows the visitor
to explore unaided or to follow a
5km waymarked circular trail
through the wood.

Visitors tempted to linger even
have the chance to stay in cabin
accommodation in the forest, with
ample opportunity to explore
further along the Devon and
Cornish coastal path and nearby
fishing villages such as Looe and
Polperro.

MAP 1

Ethy Wood
Lerryn village, Lostwithiel

From Lostwithiel on the A390 take a minor road southeast signed to Lerryn.
Park in the car park at Lerryn, and cross the River Lerryn either by the
stepping stones or by the road bridge. Head left once over the river and
walk down the north bank down a lane with cottages on either side. This
will lead to a path in the wood which follows the Lerryn and a tributary.
(SX136569), 18ha (44acres)
National Trust

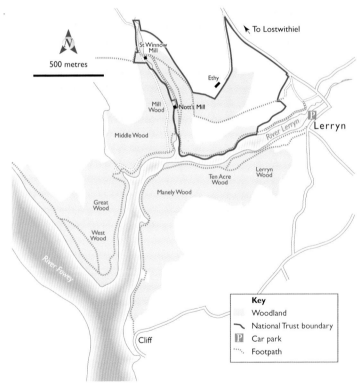

Key

	Woodland
	National Trust boundary
P	Car park
	Footpath

If you're brave, you can enjoy an exciting approach to this small, but beautiful wood – via stepping stones across the River Lerryn.

Ethy stands on the upper reaches of the River Fowey so the smell of salt is always in the air as you enjoy the views of the river's muddy banks, with oak trees almost reaching down to the river's edge.

A network of paths crisscrossing the site provides an insight into the frequent use made of it in the past. Today, they provide a choice of walks by which to explore, including a circular walk or a pretty route where the woodland edge meets the salty water of the Lerryn, and there was once a port for sailing barges.

By Lerryn Creek, the wood is young and coniferous. This was once part of the parkland of Ethy House, which descended elegantly down to the river.

From there to St Winnow Mill is ancient woodland, with oak coppice that remained uncut between World War One and the 1980s, when it was thinned to encourage it to mature into high forest. This long period of non-disturbance has produced an abundant ground flora.

The less brave-hearted can enjoy gentle strolls through this pretty site.

Ethy Wood

Milltown and Lantyan Woods

Milltown & Lantyan Woods
Milltown near Lostwithiel

Turn off A390 Lostwithiel to St Austell road onto B3269 towards Fowey. Take left signed Milltown and Castle then fork right and right again. At bottom of hill either turn left and park on roadside or turn right, park on roadside and follow footpath sign to wood. Alternatively, bear right up hill, under (low) bridge. At junction follow road uphill (do not turn right through farm) for 1.5km (1 mile). Entrance to Lantyan Wood on left with layby parking for 2 cars.
(SX110571), 33ha (82acres), AONB
Woodland Trust

Perfect for those looking to escape the crowds, this quiet woodland has a real atmosphere of tranquillity – and lovely river valley views.

It clothes the steeply sloping western side of the upper River Fowey valley but has good links to the large village of Lostwithiel and a network of tracks and paths, albeit sometimes muddy. The Saints Way passes close by.

A history of coppicing has produced a variety of size and age of tree species. Oak coppice tends to be sited on the upper plateau while elsewhere it is mostly standards within the high forest canopy. In other areas there is a mix of beech, sycamore, sweet chestnut and ash as well.

There's a good variety of ground flora, too, from bramble and bracken to wood anemone, cow wheat, woodrush and bilberry and, in spring, a dense carpet of bluebells.

Kilminorth Wood

Looe

In Looe park in large pay and display car park (Discovery Centre) on west side of the river. (SX247538), 46ha (114acres)

Caradon District Council

Scenic and atmospheric, this coastal site – the largest expanse of western oak woodland in the area – slopes steeply down to the West Looe river.

The woods are renowned for the mosses, ferns and lichens which grow in the dense and damp woodland at the foot of the slope.

Part of the Giant's Hedge, a nine-mile linear ancient monument, runs through the wood.

At low tide you can walk along the muddy shoreline to watch swans, herons, kingfishers, little egrets, gulls and cormorants feeding. Crabs, cockles and lugworms all enjoy the salty estuary environment.

Waymarked paths provide a choice of trails to explore the wood, where peregrines and buzzards circle overhead and butterflies appear in coppiced clearings. In spring your visit will be rewarded with a fine show of bluebells.

Most of the trails include steps and steep slopes, however there is a short stroll suitable for less-able visitors which leads to the riverside.

Kilminorth Wood

MAP 1

Kings Wood
London Apprentice

1.5km (1 mile) south of London Apprentice toward Pentewan on B3273. Car park and wood on left. Or immediately after Kings Wood restaurant on south edge of London Apprentice turn left, following track for 400m and then right along narrow lane. Park at end of lane near wood gates. (SX007487), 59ha (146acres)

Woodland Trust

Lying on a steep valley side of the Pentewan Valley, Kings Wood is well loved and well used by local communities, thanks in part to its prominence on the local landscape.

Visible from local homes, amenities and roads from St Austell to Mevagissey, it is a popular spot for dog walking, recreation and for people with a keen interest in the natural environment.

The area is important for birds and insects with several butterfly and moth species rare to Cornwall recorded here in recent years. The site is also notable for its rich ground flora – including bluebells – and is designated a county wildlife site.

The woods themselves are mainly mature oak with sycamore, beech, sweet chestnut, ash and birch along with areas of southern beech, larch, Douglas and Noble fir, Sitka spruce and western hemlock.

Along the valley bottom, next to the St Austell river lies an extensive section of wet, marshy woodland.

Idless Woods
Truro
From A390 in Truro, take B3284
northwest towards A30, as you
come towards the edge of town,
take turning on right signed Idless.
Go into Idless village and the
wood entrance is on the right.
(SW825483), 114ha (282acres)
Forestry Commission

The peaceful setting of Idless
Woods, along the side of the River
Allen valley, makes this a very
popular site with wildlife.

   Depending on the time of year,
there is the chance to spot red or
roe deer, otters or badgers,
and birdlife includes buzzard,
woodlark, nightjar and sparrow
hawk.

   Its proximity to the village of
Idless and the city of Truro makes
it a big hit with local people. It's a
wonderful destination for visitors
looking for a tranquil place in
which to either enjoy a gentle
stroll or explore deeper into the
heart of this mixed coniferous and
deciduous woodland of oak,
willow, rowan and hazel.

   Beautiful and graceful conifers
drape the sides of well-made forest
tracks while the banks of the rides
and tracks are teeming with
wildflowers.

MAP 1

Trelissick

Truro

From Truro take A39 south. Turn left onto B3289, Trelissick is at the end of the road before the ferry on the right.

(SW830398), 72ha (178acres), AONB, SSSI

National Trust

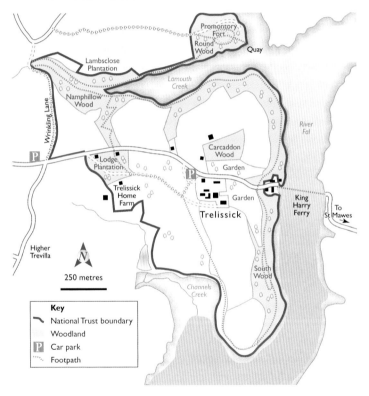

Trelissick

Take lots of time to soak up all the delights this National Trust gem, a large estate on a peninsula beside the River Fal, has to offer.

Wonderful woodland and much more is available on the Trelissick estate, including the park, garden and to a lesser extent, the house itself.

Bounded on three sides by the River Fal, the estate includes an interesting woodland walk. Hugging the water's edge, it takes in a series of natural and man-made features.

Zigzag your way down through woodland to the riverside and relax on a bench amid the trees, enjoying glimpses of Lamouth Creek and drink-in a typical Cornish estuarine landscape.

En route look out for the many water features, streams, birds, summerhouses, and the beautiful Trelissick gardens. You might glimpse seagoing ships or encounter historic remnants such as an Iron Age hill fort.

Look out too for kingfishers, redshanks and black-tailed godwits along with herons and shelduck on the river. Tree species include holly, hazel, oak, beech, and sycamore, Scots pine and larch. Pipistrelle and brown long-eared bats can been seen at dusk.

Signs of the past to keep an eye out for include wharves from where tin and copper were shipped, Roundwood Quay – once a shipbuilding base – and a malt house, lime kiln and sawpit.

Look out for remnant oak coppice – once used to produce bark for the tanning industry.

MAP 1

Tehidy Country Park
Camborne

Tehidy can be accessed from the
A30 at Camborne by heading
towards South Tehidy, and looking
for signs from there or from
Portreath take the B3301 west,
and the car park on the north side
of the site is signed off the road.
(SW640438, SW650432,
SW656440), 100ha (247acres)

Cornwall County Council

Perched right on the windswept
northern coast of Cornwall,
Tehidy is a well-used country park
with lots of good networks of
paths for exploration.

The park provides a mixture of
woodland, meadows, lakes and
ponds which support varied
wildlife.

On a stormy day the northern
section takes the brunt of the
weather, with trees bent right over
by the prevailing winds. But this
mixed deciduous woodland, which
is made up of oaks and conifers, is
a great place to take a walk with
children and dogs or on horseback
or bicycle, since it has a four-mile
network of tracks which would
suit all.

The site is surrounded by
stunning countryside and Land's
End is not too far away. It would
be possible to combine a visit to
both for a full day of discovery.

Pendarves Wood
Camborne

Heading south from Camborne on
the B3303, 1.5km (1 mile) on left.
(SW640376), 16ha (40acres)

Cornwall Wildlife Trust

You need to overcome a few
parking problems and some
slightly misleading nature trail
signs to get into and around this
site but once that's done, you can
enjoy a pleasant walk through

young woodland.

Said to be spectacular in May
when the woodland floor is
covered with bluebells, this former
parkland lies in the valley of the
River Connor and is a mixed
woodland site with sunny glades –
full of butterflies and dragonflies –
and open water.

Broadleaves, beech, sessile oak
and sycamore are found with
shrubs such as rhododendron and
cherry laurel. Dead wood has been
left to rot where it has become an
important habitat for fungi

Charcoal making

and lichens.

Part way through the site is a lake with a bench where you can relax in peaceful surroundings and watch ducks and swans. There are two nature trails to enjoy, a babbling brook and lots of woodland sounds to absorb.

Devichoys Wood
Falmouth

The entrance to the reserve is immediately after turning left to Mylor & Restronguet from the A39 in Perranarworthal, 5 km (3 miles) north of Penryn. There is a small pull-in by the reserve entrance. (SW772376), 16ha (40acres)
Cornwall Wildlife Trust

This well managed site is a great place to see heathland-loving flora – if you can tune out the rumble of traffic from the nearby A39.

Oak and hazel coppice dominates the semi-natural woodland, with birch and introduced species such as turkey oak, sycamore, beech and sweet chestnut.

The understorey has developed into mature holly woodland in places, interspersed with rowan and birch.

Work to remove rhododendron, beech and sycamore is being carried out and charcoal is produced here from timber grown on-site

Once inside, make a beeline for the lighter parts of the wood where you can find heathland type flora including heather and a beautiful layer of bilberry.

Birdspotters should look out for tree creeper, greater spotted woodpecker and mistle thrush.

Dogs must be kept on a lead.

MAP 1

Penrose Wood

Helston

From Helston take the B3304 towards Porthleven. Either park in the amenity area car park on left soon after joining the B3304 or continue for 3km (2 miles), turning left past Penrose gates and left again to sign-posted car park.

(SW639259) 96ha (237acres)

National Trust

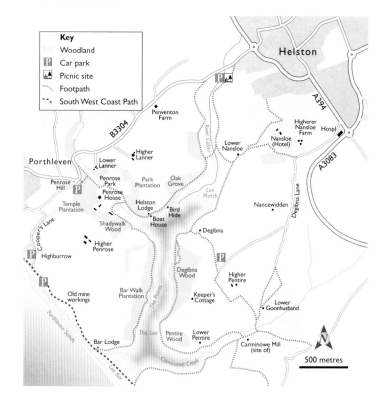

Penrose Wood

If you like your woods to be beautiful, Penrose will have you feeling like a child in a chocolate factory. It's a beautiful woodland in an amazing setting.

The woodland, which surrounds Loe Pool, Cornwall's largest freshwater lake, is very important for over-wintering wildfowl and is brimming with natural beauty, from sweeping, 19th-century parkland, through lovely oak woodland and the exhilaration of watching massive waves crashing against a shingle shore.

Loe Pool is tucked away from sight until you start to walk down the access track when the natural beauty of the site swings into view.

Public footpaths hugging the woodland edge lead from the car park to the sea, providing tantalising glimpses of the lake, marsh and the sea en route. Throughout, the senses are assaulted by the sights, sounds and smells of nature and the salty air.

Well-made tracks lead through ancient oak and wet willow and alder woods to Victorian-planted Monterey pine and cypress on the exposed cliffs of Loe Bar. It's a great place for a picnic before taking perhaps half a day or more for a slow walk covering the five-mile circumference of the Loe Pool.

The site is steeped in history, which is explained in more detail in a National Trust leaflet, which also describes walks around Penrose to discover more about its wildlife and the heritage of what is a wonderful site.

MAP 2

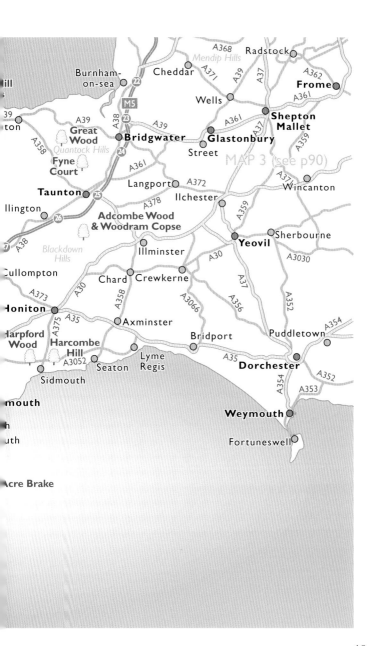

MAP 2

Arlington
Barnstaple

13km (8 miles) northeast of Barnstaple on A39. Use A39 from South Molton if travelling from the south. (SS612407),
214ha (528 acres)
National Trust

Well worth a day out, Arlington Court and the grounds and beautiful woodland that surround it are the perfect place to see nature at its varied and exciting best.

It is enveloped by graceful and elegant parklands, serviced by a network of carriageways – complete with carriage service – which include some beautiful standards of oak and sycamore dripping with lichens and ferns.

Probably dating back to the Middle Ages, the landscape retains many of its ancient features but modern management incorporates a planting programme too, including a bold young monkey puzzle avenue tempting visitors, via good signing, to head for the semi-natural woodland and into the Yeo Valley towards a lake where mallard abound.

The woodland edges are important feeding grounds for the resident horseshoe bats and visitors to the grand but unpretentious lichen-covered house can view them roosting via remote camera in a special bat 'cave'.

Arlington

Heddon Valley
Lynton

Halfway between Combe Martin
and Lynton, off A39 at Hunter's Inn.
(SS655480), 191ha (472acres), SSSI
National Trust

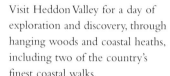

Visit Heddon Valley for a day of
exploration and discovery, through
hanging woods and coastal heaths,
including two of the country's
finest coastal walks.

Well-tended and marked paths
and bridleways meander through
woods of ash and hazel or oak and
beech, offering walkers, riders and
cyclists a choice of route. On the
coast are ravens, razorbills and
guillemots while in the woods,

pied flycatchers, wood warblers
and red deer thrive.

Climbing high, along one of
many trails, you might catch a
glimpse of heather and bracken-
covered coastal heaths through an
open canopy of ash and hazel or
oak and beech woods.
Occasionally, trees arch over
pathways, creating magical covered
ways.

Hedge banks line the valley road
– havens for flowers and ferns –
creating unforgettable borders of
texture and colour. Glossy, green
wall pennywort appears sewn into
banks of wild strawberry, red
campion, herb robert, foxglove and
hart's tongue fern.

Heddon Valley

51

MAP 2

Glenthorne

Lynton

Park at County Gate on A39 at Devon/Somerset border. Track
leading down to woods is on opposite side of the road.
(SS794487), 80ha (197acres)

Mr G Halliday

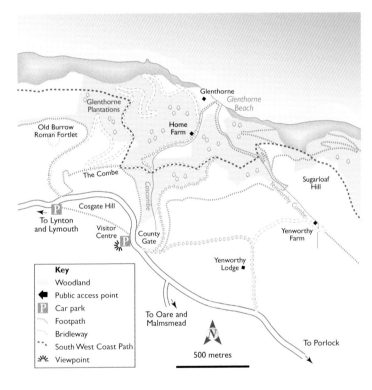

Key

- Woodland
- ◄ Public access point
- P Car park
- ········· Footpath
- ········· Bridleway
- - - - - South West Coast Path
- ※ Viewpoint

Glenthorne
Glenthorne Beach
Glenthorne Plantations
Old Burrow Roman Fortlet
Home Farm
The Combe
Coscombe
Yenworthy Combe
Sugarloaf Hill
Cosgate Hill
To Lynton and Lymouth
Visitor Centre
County Gate
Yenworthy Farm
Yenworthy Lodge
To Oare and Malmsmead
To Porlock

N

500 metres

Woodland seclusion meets wild, windy coastline at Glenthorne, which adorns a dramatic slope on the Devon/Somerset border.

A walk through this site is a wonderful experience, not least for some dramatic views across mixed mature woodland to the South Wales coast. Thanks to a very steep 1,000ft trawl, this is no visit for the faint-hearted.

Climbing steeply through mixed woodland and heath, the route gives way to mixed planting on one side of the path and mature woodland on the other, opening up at a dramatic, windy spot with wonderful vistas.

The approach to the combe is dotted with oaks above rhododendron. As the wind gusts overhead, the deep, mossy hollow offers security and seclusion – and two dramatic waterfalls – while the steep descent brings the wild coastline closer. Birdsong, meanwhile, is carried in the calm of the understorey

This is a windy spot and the prevailing wind carries the roar of Sisters' Fountain ahead to meet you.

Eventually you reach a very wild pebble and boulder beach where the sound of stones being dragged and rolled by the waves suggests bathing is not a safe bet.

To complete your woodland experience, the site provides parking, information and toilet facilities at County Gate between Easter and the end of October.

Glenthorne

MAP 2

Watersmeet

Watersmeet
Lynmouth

The National Trust car park lies just south of Lynmouth on the A39 towards Barnstaple. (SS744487), 250ha (618acres), SSSI
National Trust

Spectacular at any time of the year, this is one of the largest surviving ancient semi-natural woodlands in southwest Britain.

The woods line steep-sided river valleys at the northern edge of Exmoor National Park where Hoar Oak Water meets the East Lyn River.

Nearby villages were devastated by floods in 1952 and it is easy to imagine the effects of torrents of water pouring down the narrow river valleys.

Today, buzzards circle overhead and dippers and wagtails enjoy the river as you explore the woods which, dominated by sessile oak with a scattering of Devon whitebeam, are especially colourful in autumn.

This is one of just two spots in Britain to find Irish spurge and the barren scree slopes are ideal for lichens, while ferns and mosses grow in wetter areas.

The well-maintained paths follow the river and have quite a climb in places. But benches and picnic tables offer the chance to rest.

Hawkcombe Wood

Hawkcombe Wood
Porlock

From A39, park in Porlock and access the wood on foot from one of the various rights of way that lead into the woods.
(SS889466), 101ha (250acres), SSSI
Exmoor National Park Authority

Part of the North Exmoor site of special scientific interest and now a National Nature Reserve, this delightful oak woodland, rich in wildlife, lines the steep sides of a valley.

The mix of woodland, moor, stream and valley, accessed from a variety of good routes, make for a great visit and the lower valley reaches are particularly pretty.

Once intensively coppiced, this lovely mature woodland is home to heath fritillary butterflies, deadwood invertebrates, red wood ants and buzzards that can be spotted wheeling overhead.

The pretty hamlet of Hawkcombe is nearby and from here you can walk up into the valley, the sounds of a stream ever present.

From Whitstone Post up on Exmoor, an attractive gorse and heather-lined moorland path leads to the woods. The path dives into the woods where dappled light filters through the leaves and lichens seem to drip from the branches of old oaks.

MAP 2

Culbone & Yearnor
Porlock

Culbone can be accessed by footpath from County Gate or via Yearnor Woods, accessed by footpath starting next to Worthy Toll. County Gate (SS794487) Worthy Toll (SS857483) 183ha (452acres)

Exmoor National Park Authority

Unforgettable Culbone and Yearnor woods are part of a swathe of beautiful coastal woodland covering the North Devon cliffs, giving this Exmoor National Park site a special feel.

The Atlantic Ocean lies 500 ft below the steep, wooded coastal path and its waves can be heard pounding at the rocky shore. Once inside the woods, however, there is a calmness, enhanced by birdsong.

Well-maintained paths and rights of way provide good access for the fit and well-shod visitor, though wheelchair access is limited.

Sweet chestnut predominates in Yearnor, spiny cases creating an unusual autumn woodland floorscape. Elsewhere is birch, oak, yew, beech and a few mature conifers. Holly and rowan create a mid-story above ground cover of greater woodrush, bramble, honeysuckle and herbs.

Pass by beautiful Culbone Church, taking the path signed 'alternative permitted coast path to Lynmouth' to Culbone, with its superb vistas through the woodland canopy to the sea and South Wales beyond.

Culbone

North Hill Woods
Minehead

Follow directions from Minehead.
(SS949468), 84ha (208acres), SSSI
Exmoor National Park Authority

This is the perfect place to sample many typical features of Exmoor National Park – in a walk.

The woods are a rich mix of natural and introduced trees, managed to offer people and wildlife the maximum benefit.

This includes keeping fallen trees as habitats where insects, birds and mammals can thrive, and leaving large specimen trees – including Corsican pine, western red cedar and Douglas fir – to add aesthetic value.

It is hoped that deer, foxes, badgers, bats and birds will all flourish as the woods evolve.

North Hill, part of a five-mile sandstone ridge includes a host of interesting archaeological features, from prehistoric barrows and the remains of medieval farms to remnants of World War Two when the ridge was used by allied troops for training.

Beyond the woods is pretty Exmoor heathland with bell heathers, gorse, scattered trees and Exmoor ponies – and views across the Bristol Channel and the woodland-draped Vale of Porlock.

North Hill Woods

Horner Wood

Porlock

From A39, 1.5km (1 mile) east of Porlock, follow signs to Luccombe, and then Horner Green.

(SS897455), 353ha (872acres), SSSI

National Trust

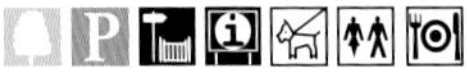

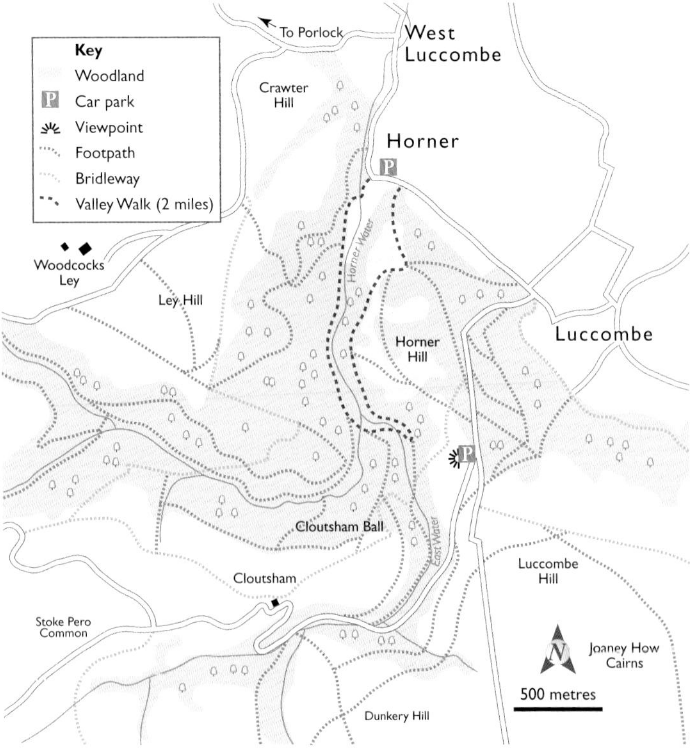
To Porlock
West Luccombe
Key
Woodland
Car park
Viewpoint
Footpath
Bridleway
Valley Walk (2 miles)
Crawter Hill
Horner
Horner Water
Woodcocks Ley
Ley Hill
Horner Hill
Luccombe
Cloutsham Ball
East Water
Cloutsham
Luccombe Hill
Stoke Pero Common
Joaney How Cairns
500 metres
Dunkery Hill

Horner Wood

This ancient woodland, part of the Dunkery and Horner Wood National Nature Reserve, is one of the largest wooded nature reserves in England.

It has an open feel – easily appreciated from any one of many routes from delightful Horner Green.

One is perfect for young families and the sound of the river accompanies you through ash and ancient hazel coppiced woodland. Once over the first stone bridge, the woods opens up and large, crowded oaks dominate.

Inside, wildlife flourishes and a good covering of ground flora includes yellow pimpernel, opposite-leaved golden saxifrage, wood sorrel and violets. No fewer than 440 different fungi, 84 of them considered rare, can be found here along with 240 species of lichen – a sign of how pure and humid the air is. Little wonder the site is referred to as rainforest.

The wood is also nationally important for the wide range of bat species that roost and feed within it – at least 14 of the 16 British bat species including the rare barbastelle.

MAP 2

Luccombe &
Chapel Plantations
Minehead

From A39, via Luccombe and
Horner Green. Webber's Post car
park is an excellent starting point
to the easy access trail.
(SS906448), 156ha (386acres), SSSI

National Trust

Spectacular moorland views, pretty
woodland and a choice of quiet,
well-maintained routes make this a
great place for anyone –
particularly older and less able
visitors – to get maximum
pleasure.

Below Webber's Post, conifer
plantations divided by the main
road, are Luccombe Plantation to
the east and Chapel Plantation to
the west. Continuous-cover
forestry can be seen in practice
with Douglas fir, Japanese larch,
western hemlock and Scots pine
mixing with oak, birch and sweet
chestnut to form attractive,
biodiverse and useful woodland.

The woods lead through to
heath pasture providing various
habitats while moorland tops
surrounding Horner Wood are
dotted with cairns and barrows,
lending an ancient feel.

Webber's Post is an excellent
starting point for exploration of
several good walking and riding
routes. Dotted with wind-sculpted
pines, it opens onto spectacular
scenery.

One very pretty walk takes a
steep downward path through
lovely old woodland before
crisscrossing the East Water via five
footbridges, emerging at
picturesque Allercombe Meadows.

Barle Valley, Hawkridge & Tarr Steps woods
Dulverton

Follow signs to Hawkridge from Dulverton and park in village. Barle Valley can be accessed from Marsh Bridge, East Ansty Common. For Tarr Steps follow signs and park in ENPA car park.
(SS861306) (SS907289) (SS870291), 100ha (247acres)
Exmoor National Park Authority

Imagine walking between ancient, lanky lichen-clad oaks illuminated by flickering daylight blinking through the treetops, to the accompaniment of river sounds....

A beautiful wildlife haven that includes moorland fringe, common land and the pretty River Barle which meanders its way down to the delightful town of Dulverton.

The woods provide a rich ecosystem which supports lichens, dormice, otters, birds and a number of invertebrates, including butterflies. It also bears testimony to a rich history with mysterious Bronze Age barrows and ancient tracks and relics – including the country's oldest clapper bridge, the 70m long Tarr Steps – which punctuate the landscape.

It's a great place for walkers, riders and cyclists alike, with a good network of footpaths and bridleways and ample viewpoints offering views across the valley.

Barle Valley

61

MAP 2

Burridge Wood
Dulverton

Park in riverside car park, Dulverton and walk across the Barle Bridge, turn sharp right signed 'Beech Tree Cross 1½, Hawkridge 4½, Tarr Steps 6'. Follow this road and at sharp corner take footpath signed ahead into woods. (SS912278), 21ha (47 acres) SSSI

Exmoor National Park Authority

The sound of the River Barle is ever present on a walk through Burridge Woods, in Exmoor National Park – part of the Barle Valley complex of ancient oak woodland.

The river rushes over boulders, providing a good habitat for otters and river birds such as the dipper.

A mixture of old sessile oak coppice, beech and birch with a hazel and holly understorey line a network of paths, and produce a rich mosaic of dappled light.

The footpath climbs very steeply, levelling out onto a wide hillside track with excellent views through the canopy to Dulverton church tower. There are great footpath links between Dulverton Woods, Hawkridge/Barle Valley and to the nearby ancient 'clapper bridge' of Tarr Steps.

An old hazel coppice near the entrance rises to meet towering high oaks with a rich holly layer beneath. Bilberry and hard fern thrives at ground level and a variety of mosses abound in damper patches.

Great Wood
Bridgewater

Heading west along A39 from Bridgewater, turn into Nether Stowey village, and follow either brown tourist signs or white fingerpost signs to Ramscombe through the small lanes. Drive along the forest track ignoring small parking areas until reaching car park at Ramscombe. (ST175375), 629ha (1555acres) AONB

Forestry Commission

There is so much to explore and discover in this extensive and wonderfully accessible woodland clothing the steep-sided combes of the Quantock Hills

Those who reach the top are rewarded with some wonderful views.

Car parks dotted throughout the site and an extensive network of rides and footpaths make it easy for visitors to explore the varied woodland habitats where red deer, badgers and a variety of birds from pied flycatchers and redstarts to wood warblers and sparrow hawks have made their homes.

The once oak-dominated woods were used to supply timber for ships and charcoal.

Much of this was replanted with larch, Sitka and Douglas fir, though there are still areas of sessile oak and beech.

In and around the Ramscombe car park, majestic Douglas fir soar above younger trees, making a striking sight against a clear blue sky. Further north, stunted oaks clothe the hillside in further contrast with their lofty stems.

Fyne Court
Taunton

From Taunton, travel through Kingston St Mary 6.5km (4 miles), to junction at top of hill, signed Fyne Court. Turn left after phone box, entrance 100m down lane on left.
(ST223322), 10ha (25acres)
Somerset Wildlife Trust

Wonderful big old beeches make attractive landmarks in this mixed wood, part of the Victorian gardens and grounds surrounding Fyne Court, until recently Somerset Wildlife Trust's headquarters.

Another interesting feature is a remnant ornamental pond, used for local school wildlife studies, which complements a walled garden and glasshouse remains.

Access is via a mainly good, though occasionally muddy path, which allows you to explore the wood through a choice of walks.

Five Pond Wood walk is particularly pleasant, leading through the gardens and across a pasture field with a fantastic, massive old ash coppice. Follow the course of a stream beneath mixed broadleaf woodland, across a field and past the church. You will encounter a mixture of large old trees and new planting on the way – perfect for families.

MAP 2

Adcombe Wood & Woodram Copse
Taunton

Follow B3170 south of Taunton. In Corfe, after right turn signed Pitminster, turn next right into Adcombe Lane towards Feltham. Follow single track lane with passing places for 2km (1 mile) up hill. Parking for 2 cars in front of wood entrance on this lane.
(ST225174), 36ha (89 acres)
AONB, SSSI
Woodland Trust

This steeply sloping wood is part of the scarp woodlands overlooking Taunton Vale in the Blackdown Hills Area of Outstanding Natural Beauty.

The wood is part of a site of special scientific interest, thanks to some fine examples of broadleaf trees for which the area is noted.

Mainly high forest, with small areas of coppice and scrub woodland, here you can see ancient woodland, oaks planted in the 19th century, and abandoned common land, now dominated by dense patches of hawthorn.

The grass field at the southern end is a great place for butterflies and a variety of plants.

The wood is served by an extensive network of rides, linking in with the surrounding countryside, but visitors should note that some of the paths and rides are very steep, and may be wet and uneven underfoot.

Harcombe Hill
Harcombe

Travelling east on A3052 through Sidmouth, take left to Harcombe after the Blue Bull Inn. After 500m turn right through Harcombe Village. Turn left up hill and, on a sharp right-hand bend, turn down track on right to car park.
(SY157909) 42ha (104 acres)
Fountain Forestry

Birdsong and the lapping of a distant stream add atmosphere and interest for visitors to Harcombe Hill, a mixed woodland in the heart of stunning Devon countryside.

While one section of the wood is ancient, Douglas fir, Japanese larch, Corsican pine, lodgepole pine and Sitka spruce planted in the 1980s dominate elsewhere.

A clockwise walk from the car park takes the visitor across open heath – with some stunning views across Sidmouth and the sea. Providing a greater challenge is the one-mile circular walk which can be hard going in places, with some steep slopes.

There is a second viewpoint about half way round the site, overlooking the valley with an area of young planted broadleaves below.

Harpford Wood
Newton Poppleford

On A3052 Exeter to Lyme Regis road, turn north at Bowd opposite B3176 road to Sidmouth. Park (400m) on left next to recycling centre.
(SY105906), 63ha (156acres)

Clinton Devon Estates

A slightly unkempt entrance belies the beauty and atmosphere of Harpford Wood.

The wood gets better the deeper you explore. A blend of different conifers – Douglas fir, Japanese larch and western hemlock – contrasts strikingly with grand old oaks and beech that stand out among other broadleaves.

The site is divided by a disused railway line which accounts for a series of Victorian brick structures dotted throughout.

Two waymarked trails are laid out with the one leading to the left of the entrance recommended (markers on the other trail are scarce in places) past a lovely stream, complete with waterfall.

Access is a little limited, since there are some very steep slopes and the paths can become boggy in sections.

If you are keen to explore further, follow the footpath to Beacon Hill.

MAP 2

Stoke Wood
Exeter

Head north from Exeter along the A396 Tiverton road. 1.5km (1 mile) after Cowley Bridge turn right into signed car park. (SX919959), 38ha (94 acres), SSSI
Forestry Commission

A haven on the very edge of suburbia, this is an important wildlife woodland on the outskirts of Exeter city and just a short drive from Tiverton.

Stoke Wood lies on a steep hillside – there are some wonderful views from the top – and it teems with birds, mammals, butterflies, insects and reptiles and even glow worms. Dormice can also be found here.

A good network of paths leads you through the wood, beneath mature oaks and areas of conifer.

There are two trails. The longer one has lovely views across the River Exe and local countryside. The shorter walk is promoted as a good way of introducing families to woodland wildlife. Exeter City Council's ranger service organises events and guided walks on the site.

Buzzards
Tiverton

From A396 Exeter to Tiverton road, go through Tiverton taking the B3137 west to Withleigh. Take first left after Withleigh Farm down narrow road. Keep going to National Trust car park on left. (SS906117), 46ha (113 acres)
National Trust

Buzzards

Imagine stepping into a rural idyll of yesteryear and you may well conjure up this fantastic woodland in the heart of the River Dart valley.

Just two miles from the pretty market town of Tiverton, Buzzards is a beautiful mixed woodland capturing the essence of the mid-Devon landscape.

Named at the wish of former owner Mr Matteson it recalls the birds he and wife Vera used to watch soaring over the valley and which still echo overhead today.

This diverse site features two woods, Thongsleigh and Huntland and includes steep pasture and water meadow.

Eggesford Wood
Chulmleigh

Follow Forestry Commission signs off A377, 19km (12 miles) northwest of Crediton.
(SS694106), 222ha (549 acres)
Forestry Commission

Eggesford Wood

With majestic, 100ft conifers swaying gently in the breeze, this tree-lined valley offers plenty of opportunities for exploration and is popular with locals.

The site is easy to access, thanks to its position next to the A377. However, this does have drawbacks since the birdsong that fills the woods is accompanied by traffic noise from the busy Bideford to Crediton road that stays with you up to half a mile into the woods, detracting somewhat from their tranquility.

Tracks and paths are well maintained and there is one trail that would suit less-able walkers. Well-spaced trees along the first part of each trail offer pleasing glimpses across the valley.

Visitors looking to extend their visit can explore part of the nearby long-distance Tarka Trail.

MAP 2

Halsdon
Dolton

From B3220 take turning to
Dolton opposite garage at Dolton
Beacon. Go through Dolton, take
first right up Fore Street, past
Royal Oak pub, continue down
West Lane to crossroads. Turn
right and use either car park on
left or continue for about 1.5km
(1 mile) and turn left down track
with Devon Wildlife Trust sign and
park in car park (400m).
(SS554131), 35ha (87 acres), SSSI
Devon Wildlife Trust

A favourite haunt of otters, for
which the River Torridge is

Halsdon

famed, Halsdon is a compact and delightful reserve, with the Tarka Trail nipping its edges.

Otters are tempted into the woods by sensitive management. The river, which meanders through part of the site, is powerful and exciting to walk beside in its own right.

A new series of well-marked trails lead through a variety of habitats in this varied, oak-dominated woodland. You might see a dipper skim the river surface, catch sight of a kingfisher or hear the shrill cry of a jay.

Grey squirrels are a common sight and overhead you might hear a buzzard. In spring, pied flycatchers and great spotted woodpeckers can be seen.

The woodland floor is richly carpeted – in autumn with herbs such as red campion and woundwort and in spring with bluebells, wild garlic, bugle and violet.

Abbeyford Woods
Okehampton
From Okehampton town centre follow signs for North Road Industrial Estate. Turn right at T junction, then first left (signposted Hook) and follow road to top of hill and main Abbeyford car park. (SX588976), 85ha (210 acres)
Forestry Commission

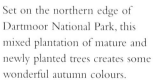

Set on the northern edge of Dartmoor National Park, this mixed plantation of mature and newly planted trees creates some wonderful autumn colours.

Areas of beech, oak, larch, Douglas fir and sweet chestnut have created a diverse combination of wildlife habitats.

As a result, the woods are frequented by red and roe deer, badgers and otters as well as numerous birds from the redstart and pied flycatcher to nightjar, buzzard and raven.

The open clearings attract insects and reptiles such as adders, which can be seen sunning themselves, and butterflies including the silver-washed fritillary.

A quiet country lane bisecting the wood forms part of the 180-mile Tarka Trail, which is popular with long-distance walkers. Those less ambitious can enjoy wandering through the wood via a series of level, well-surfaced paths, which are ideal for less able visitors and pushchairs. Other, steeper paths offer views across to Dartmoor and Okehampton.

MAP 2

Castle Drogo Estate
Moretonhampstead

Take A382 Whiddon Down to
Moretonhampstead road; turn off
at Sandy Park and follow signs.
(SX721900) 329ha (813 acres), SSSI
National Trust

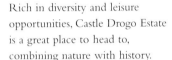

Rich in diversity and leisure
opportunities, Castle Drogo Estate
is a great place to head to,
combining nature with history.

Dominated by sessile oak
woodlands with some large beech
trees lining the valley bottom, the
steep-sided woodland includes
conifer plantations, which add to
the mix and give rise to some

wonderful walks.

One route follows the Dunsford
path through the River Teign valley
woodlands, alongside the river
which forms a natural focal point.
The bright-blue flash of kingfishers
adds to the cocktail of wildlife
here. Another route flows through
Rectory and Drewston Woods,
offering fantastic views over the
valley and across to the distant
heath.

Heathland and Iron Age forts add
natural and historical interest.
Whiddon Deer Park, which sits
below Castle Drogo, is a designated
site of special scientific interest
because of its rich variety of lichens.

Castle Drogo

Dunsford Wood
Dunsford

Take the A382 from Bovey Tracey to Moretonhampstead and then the B3212 from Moretonhampstead to Exeter. Dunsford Wood is at Steps Bridge just before you reach Dunsford. Entrance to reserve on left after Steps Bridge.
(SX805884), 57ha (141 acres), SSSI
Devon Wildlife Trust

Renowned for its display of spring daffodils – said to be the best in the county – this wood is also a great place to enjoy bluebells.

Teeming with wildlife, including six types of fritillary butterflies and numerous birds, deer, dormice and otters, it also boasts the elusive kingfisher, while salmon and sea trout swim through the waters of the River Teign.

Enjoyment is by no means restricted to wildlife and human visitors can take their pick of walks along well-maintained paths through the woods and along other sections of the Teign Valley.

Oak trees cloak the steep valley sides, many lichen-encrusted. Areas of hazel coppice and ash can be found, mainly along the valley bottom where you will discover glades of wild daffodils.

Dunsford Wood

MAP 2

Teign Valley Woods

Teign Valley Woods
Moretonhampstead

5km (3 miles) northeast of Moretonhampstead, take the winding B3212 towards Exeter for a further 5km (3 miles) until you reach the car park just before Steps Bridge.
(SX803884), 111ha (275 acres) SSSI
National Trust

From spring daffodils to summer foxgloves, autumn bilberries to winter snowdrops, there is year-round colour and interest in Teign Valley Woods.

This is a magnificent woodland complex, stretching along the banks of the river – with ample opportunities for walking, be it a short stroll or longer exploration.

Mainly oak, with hazel, birch and bracken beneath, the woods are served by a well-maintained network of paths, some of them rising steeply above the Teign – the constant relaxing river sounds never far away.

Kingfishers thrive here, along with pied flycatchers and redstart. Butterflies – including the high-brown fritillary – also make this their home and there are wood-ant nests in abundance.

A large area of oak woodland, as well as open valley meadows beside the river, add to the site's diversity.

Fernworthy Forest
Chagford

Following the A383 Moretonhamstead to Okehampton road, take the B3206 to Chagford. From Chagford centre take left signposted Fernworthy Reservoir and follow to the reservoir. (SX668838) 590ha (1458 acres)

Forestry Commission & South West Lakes Trust

What a combination – wild moorland, reservoir, forest and fantastic views, all waiting to be enjoyed in the space of a visit.

All this is spiced up with a helping of history, in the form of stone circles and stone rows that you pass as you follow the path through this wonderful wood.

Fernworthy Forest is a fantastic location and great for walks on sunny early autumn days, when you can really enjoy the colours of the berries, coconut-smelling gorse flowers and bright bracken.

The site is dominated by even-aged conifers, Sitka spruce, Douglas fir and Japanese larch. This is very much a working wood so look out for signs of felling and replanting. There are some particularly large and handsome firs and spruce dotted along the sides of the stream.

Access is good, generally, with the odd patch of boggy ground and some steep sections to be aware of.

MAP 2

Wray Cleave
Moretonhampstead

From Bovey Tracey take the A382 towards Moretonhampstead, after 6.5km (4 miles) there is a small layby on right, and a stile leading into the adjoining wood.
(SX775837), 31ha (74 acres)
Dartmoor National Park Authority

Stout footwear and a good sense of direction are ideal companions on a visit to this 'wild' yet peaceful wood on Dartmoor's edge.

From the layby, follow the path until you see a stile over a wall into Wray Cleave to the north. Alternatively there is access into the

northern end of the wood at Pepperdon Mine, or from the east on footpath 23 from Pepperdon Common.

Dominated by bracken on the upper slope and dotted with abandoned mine workings, the path can sometimes be difficult to follow. But perseverance pays off since, on the upper reaches, some wonderful old oak pollards spread out in open and sunny glades. Birdlife abounds in this ridge-top haven, where no other sound penetrates.

The visitor is treated to occasional glimpses of Dartmoor through the oak, ash and sycamore trees. Beneath the canopy, hazel and holly provide autumn nuts and bright winter berries.

A good, level track runs along the bottom of the wood where yellow spots on trees help guide visitors along the public footpath. There are other permissive paths but these are not marked.

An undulating carpet of bluebells in the southwest corner indicates a former ridge and furrow site. At the northeast end the remains of intensive mining activity is evident.

As the wood hugs a fairly steep slope and some of the paths are overgrown, exploration can be a challenge.

Wray Cleave

Shaptor Woods
Bovey Tracey

Turn left in Bovey Tracey High Street by town hall and into Mary Street. Right at hospital up Furzeleigh Lane, wood on left. Furzeleigh Wood entrance also offers parking but is restricted. (SX819798), 79ha (195 acres)

Woodland Trust

Shaptor Woods

Shaptor Woods, a large expanse of woodland made up of a series of smaller, semi-natural ancient woodland sites, are a local landmark on Dartmoor's southeastern side.

They line the upper slopes of the Wray Valley, and link with a number of other woods to form an extensive site, surrounded by a mixture of grassland and arable fields.

Much of the woodland covers former moor 'waste' land but its most striking characteristic is an abundance of granite boulders which lie strewn across the woodland floor. These are at their most impressive near Shaptor Rocks.

While the area is renowned for its upland oak woodland, there are also small areas which favour flora that is more characteristic of a lowland mixed-broadleaf wood. Many ancient field boundaries can be seen throughout the woods.

Within the site are an abundance of mature, open-grown veteran trees encrusted with bryophytes and lichens which also cling to the exposed granite boulders and old walls.

The area was once mined for iron-oxide ore and remnants of the industry can still be found.

There are two public rights of way and a permissive path leading onto Shaptor Rocks where the visitor can enjoy magnificent views across the local landscape, a patchwork of grassland and arable fields.

MAP 2

Parke Estate
Bovey Tracey

From the A38 Exeter to Plymouth road, take the A382 towards Bovey Tracey. At second roundabout turn left towards Widecombe, after 400m turn right into Parke Estate.
(SX806785), 51ha (126acres)
National Trust

Adorning the steep sides of the River Bovey valley, these woods are part of a larger estate which beckons to be explored, its mix of woodland, valley meadows, open parkland and orchard providing lots of interest.

Made up of oak, ash, sweet chestnut and sycamore, along with areas of beech and conifers, the woods are explored via long easy, gently sloping paths rising up the steep wooded valley side. Here and there, viewpoints offer outstanding views across the woods and beyond.

It is possible to form a circular route by crossing the river and walking back along the disused Haylor tramway.

Kingfishers and dippers hunt for food along the river while the meadows host wonderful June displays of common spotted and summer marsh orchids, with brimstone butterflies in summer. A 17th-century mill leat and weir feed a fishpond favoured these days by moorhens and mallards.

Parke Estate

Grey Park Wood
Ashburton

Turn off A38 at Pear Tree Junction, follow to town centre. Turn left into North Street then left at end into Headborough Road. Follow to village of Buckland in the Moor 5km (3 miles). Entrance to wood on left opposite pretty thatched cottages by a stream.
(SX721727), 15ha (37acres)
AONB, SSSI
Woodland Trust

Situated on the southeastern flank of Dartmoor, this pretty site is dominated by oak high forest dating back to the early 1800s. It is part of a large complex known as the Holne Woodlands.

The wood is bisected by Ruddycleave Water, a fast-flowing stream, which becomes a small gorge in places. As it descends, the stream passes through massive granite boulders, creating an impressive feature and humid conditions in which lush plant communities thrive.

At its northern end the wood changes from mature beech, sycamore and ash to larch and Douglas fir above a wet, boggy woodland floor. The understorey has been cleared to improve conditions for lichens, for which this wood is famed.

The old estate track that runs the length of Ruddycleave Water is bounded in places by well-crafted stone walls and culverts. It is unclear whether the clapper bridge which forges the stream is ancient or a more modern feature.

MAP 2

Great Plantation
Bovey Tracey

From Bovey Tracey A382 northbound take left onto road signposted Liverton and Coldeast. After 1.5km (1 mile) woodland on left. There are two entrances with parking opportunities.
(SX814752), 200ha (494acres)
Forestry Commission

Surrounded on three sides by road, including the busy A38, it comes as a wonderful surprise to explore Great Plantation and discover a delightfully interesting woodland.

Particularly colourful in autumn, the 200 hectare site is very diverse, with areas of heath, broadleaf-lined stream sections and tall conifer stands. It is mainly coniferous plantation but there are lots of broadleaves along the pathways and stream sides.

Explore deeper, the sounds of traffic fade and you find yourself on a heath with natural regeneration of pine and birch, heather, bilberry and bracken that lends a very natural feel.

The 18-mile Templer Way runs through, following the route by which granite was exported from Dartmoor via the Haytor Granite Tramway and Stover canal.

Access is good, thanks to lots of flat, informal paths. They can get very wet so wellies and waterproof trousers are recommended.

Stover Country Park
Bovey Tracey

Turn off the A38 at the Bovey
Tracey/Newton Abbot junction,
taking the A382 towards Newton
Abbot, almost immediately turn
left into Stover Country Park
(SX835751) 46ha (114acres), SSSI
Devon County Council

The main feature of this easily
accessed and popular country park
is its large man-made lake
surrounded by mixed woodland.
This includes an arboretum,
pinetum and an aerial walkway –
a hit with children – introducing
information about woods and
their wildlife in novel ways. A bird
hide offers the chance for quiet
observation.

Other wildlife residents in the
wood include roe deer, dormice,
white admiral butterflies, spotted
flycatchers and tawny owls.

A well-surfaced lakeside path,
well populated with benches, gives
visitors the chance to enjoy picnics
or frequent stops to watch the
constant bird activity on the lake.

A long-distance walk, the
Templar Way, runs through the
park. Part of it helps form a
circular trail.

Stover Country Park

MAP 2

White Wood Holne
Holne / Ashburton

From Ashburton follow the B3357 towards Princetown. Fork left on Newbridge Hill towards Holne village. Continue past village until you reach Vennford Dam. Cross over dam and car park on right. (SX685713), 66ha (163acres)

Dartmoor National Park Authority

If you have ever wished to see a fantastic ancient oak coppice woodland, make a beeline for White Wood.

You can enter the wood along different routes. From the car park you can walk behind the quarry area and then fork right and cross a small stream, to follow a level, stony pipeline track or head north across the moor to an old packhorse track which leads to the wood and river.

Further paths into the wood can be accessed from open moor around Bench Tor.

Thanks to its pollution-free environment and remote location on the steep sides of the upper River Dart valley, the wood has survived to sustain a population of nationally important lichens and mosses.

It also boasts some spectacular views across the wood and river, while within there is a chance to appreciate a mix of oak, hazel, and birch with a ground cover including woodruff, primrose, bilberry and heather.

5,000 years of human occupation locally add interest for the visitor. The surrounding moorland contains ample evidence of prehistoric dwellings, medieval field systems and burial cairns.

White Wood Holne

Holne Woods
Ashburton

Leave the A38 at the Ashburton junction. Follow the road towards Dartmeet/Princetown (B3357) for 6.5km (4 miles) until you reach a large car park at Newbridge. Cross back over river on the stone bridge and turn right to enter Holne Wood.
(SX711708), 66ha (163acres), SSSI
National Trust

Part of Dartmoor's largest stretch of native oak woodland, this is a beautiful site by the River Dart and is popular with families for picnics and paddling.

Beyond the river's edge you discover some stunning views and a wonderful calm. Within this deep wooded valley live deer, pied flycatchers, redstarts, goosanders, dragonflies and dippers.

The oak woodland, once coppiced for charcoal burning, has a carpet of gorse, ferns and mosses. A firm path leads visitors far above the fast-flowing river where salmon spawn provide a tasty treat for otters, and white-water rapids attract canoeists.

A medieval three-span packhorse bridge straddles the river at Newbridge, where, unlike most of Dartmoor the ground is slate, forged by the heat generated by the molten magma which formed the region 295 million years ago.

Holne Woods forms part of the Dart Prime Biodiversity Area – a section of moorland, rivers, farms and woodland of international importance to wildlife.

Holne Woods

MAP 2

Hembury Woods
Buckfastleigh

From the A38 Buckfastleigh
junction follow signs towards
Buckfast Abbey. Just after the
abbey entrance take next right
signposted Buckfast. Follow road
out of Buckfast towards Holne and
Scorriton. After 400m turn right,
signposted Hembury Woods, to
car park. (SX729680)
105ha (260acres), SSSI
National Trust

Hembury Woods

A spectacular location on the
slopes of an Iron Age hill fort
make Hembury Woods an
atmospheric place to explore.

A mix of woodland, scrub, heath
and pasture creates a diverse array
of habitats, particularly for the mix
of invertebrates and lichens that
thrive here. Winter residents
include greater and lesser
horseshoe bats.

Both parking and picnicking can
be enjoyed in attractive settings
before taking a walk along
occasionally steep paths through
oak, birch and an understorey of
holly, hazel and gorse.

In spring there is an abundance
of bluebells to enjoy and later on,
honeysuckle, woodrush, bilberry
and common cow wheat bring
colour and interest.

As you wend your way through
the wood you eventually reach the
highest point – the fort. From this
open area you can take in the
surrounding Dartmoor
countryside.

Scadson/Ten Acre Brake
Paignton

At Five Lanes roundabout on the
A3022 Torbay ring road turn into
Preston Down Road. After 250m
turn left into Cockinton Lane. After
a short drive, entrance on right.

(SX884634), 35ha (87acres)
Torbay Council

Once part of the large Cockington
Estate, this peaceful wood provides

a 'green lung' for people living in the nearby residential area.

Beneath the mix of ash, oak and sycamore grow unusually named plants such as town hall clock and alternate-leaved golden saxifrage.

Coppicing, a common practice here at one time, has been reintroduced and the woodland today generates products such as thatching spurs and bean poles.

Traces of its history can still be seen in the shape of remnants from a Victorian pumping system, once used to take water from the river and over the hill to irrigate the fields around Cockington.

Explore via a series of level paths that lead by the river. A circular route links with nearby Occombe Wood, see next entry.

Another option is a visit to the 460 acre Cocking Country Park, with its 17th-century house, crafts, rose garden, organic kitchen garden and countryside walks.

Occombe Wood
Paignton

At Five Lanes roundabout on the A3022 Torbay ring road turn into Preston Down Road. After 250m a public right of way on right gives access to the wood.
(SX874632), 27ha (67acres)
Torbay Council

Once owned, according to the Domesday Book, by the Bishops of Exeter, today's Occombe Wood – 'Valley of the Oaks' – is a pretty nature reserve set amongst housing.

Popular with local walkers, the wood lines a steep-sided valley and contains ancient oaks, ash, hazel and holly along with a wealth of ground flora including wood sorrel, pignut and yellow archangel.

A stream running at the bottom of the valley has created a damp environment in which ferns, mosses and lichens thrive.

If you're interested in extending your visit, a waymarked route takes you on a two-hour circular walk through Occombe and neighbouring Scadson Wood (see previous entry). East of here, an area of open grassland offers fine views of Paignton and the coastline, which also boasts some enjoyable walks.

Or you could call at neighbouring Occombe Farm where the Torbay Coast and Countryside Trust is developing a demonstration farm with visitor facilities.

MAP 2

Marridge/Elberry/ The Grove Woods
Brixham

Head south from Paignton on the A3022 Dartmouth road. Bear right at 'Windy Corner' traffic lights and immediately left into Bascombe Road. After 1.5km (1 mile) turn left at T junction, and just after the road bears right there is an access track on the left. Walk down access track for 500m to reach the wood. (SX905563)
46ha (114ACRES), AONB
Torbay Council

Perfect for a short stroll or longer circular route, this trio of woods is perched on a headland with pretty views across the sea and a stream of boats to watch in this busy coastal area.

The Grove is an ancient wood, though it has been planted more recently with larch and sweet chestnut. But you can find bluebells, butcher's broom and spindle here. Look out for the remains of limekilns which once produced quicklime in seven limestone quarries along this stretch of coastline.

Leading through Churstone Cove, where the views open out, the coastal path continues through Marridge Wood into Elberry, a narrow stretch of woodland which spills down the cliff below. It's a mix of mature beech and sweet chestnut.

Two nearby shingle coves and a pretty stretch of white shingle beach at Elberry Cove means picnic and paddling make the perfect complement to your woodland walk.

Elberry

Lukesland Cleave
Ivybridge

From Ivybridge cross over the
railway and head north towards
Harford for 500m soon after
Ermewood House turn down
access track (with open field gate)
to small parking area.
(SX640576), 17ha (42acres)
Mrs R Howell, Lukesland Estate

Lukesland Cleave

This is a hidden gem, lying on the
wooded slopes of the River Erme
valley where the river
environment creates a wonderful
habitat for damp-loving ferns and
mosses while dippers enjoy
fishing.

   Privately owned Lukesland
Cleave includes a conifer
plantation of Douglas fir, larch,
western red cedar and mixed
woodland of oak, ash and some
ancient beech. Look closer and
you'll discover exotic species –
including towering redwood,
monkey puzzle and Noble fir
planted over a hundred years ago.

   A steep zigzag path leads down
to the pretty, fast-flowing Erme as
it is channeled through narrow
rocky sections of river bed. Small
waterfalls and foaming torrents
cascade down river through the
rapids while, further downstream,
the river widens dramatically and
there is ample opportunity to
picnic on the nearby rocks.

   Deer, badger, buzzards and
woodcock are just some of the
residents here.

MAP 2

Hardwick Wood
Plympton

In Plympton follow signs for Plymstock. Turn right into Merafield Road. Just after entrance to Saltram House (NT) and before Merafield Road crosses the A38 pull onto wide verge on left by main entrance gate.
(SX530556), 22ha (54acres)

Woodland Trust

A local landmark, Hardwick Wood sits atop a hill on the outskirts of Plympton village and Plymouth City.

Hardwick Wood

It's a wonderful place for springtime visits, when visitors can enjoy a superb show of bluebell, ransom and campion.

Broadleaved trees dominate this ancient woodland site which features two areas of contrasting character.

In its windblown central section the mature tree canopy is thin with young trees underplanted to regenerate those lost in the gales, while the more sheltered eastern end of the wood was affected very little and the woods maintain oak, ash and beech high forest.

A network of green rides crisscross the site, which, along with a network of narrow paths, provides its visitors with a variety of routes to explore.

Ermington Wood
Ivybridge

From Ermington village take the A3121 towards Ugborough. As you leave the village turn first right after Kingsacre nursing home, then right again up a steep access track to small parking area.
(SX643529), 23ha (56acres)
Flete Estate

A delight. That's one way to sum up Ermington Wood, which lines the slopes of a rural valley close to the South Harns coastline and boasts some lovely views across the local landscape.

This is a great place for a family walk, thanks to its manageable size and three well-marked trails which guide the visitor along wide access tracks.

Benches are strategically placed to allow time to enjoy the delightful views across to Ermington village and the surrounding hills, from where Dartmoor rises up beyond.

The wood was planted in the 1950s and consists mainly of beech and western hemlock while some oak and birch are regenerating naturally. The site is being managed today with some areas felled and replanted with species that include sweet chestnut.

It's possible to combine this with a seaside treat by visiting the nearby beaches of Wonwell or Mothecombe.

Andrew's Wood

Andrew's Wood
Loddiswell

From the A38 follow the A3121
towards Ugborough and
Yealmpton. At the crossroads go
straight on towards Modbury
(B3196). At California Cross fork
left after petrol station towards
Loddiswell. Car park on right
approximately 150m after
Coldharbour Cross.
(SX713520)
28ha (81acres), AONB
Devon Wildlife Trust

This delightful Devon nature
reserve is perfect for a family day
out, as it is easily combined with
nearby Blackdown Rings hill fort,
Avon Woods and scenic Loddiswell.

A blend of open meadows and
wet woodland, its network of
boardwalks and bridges allows
visitors easy access and fine views
of Dartmoor's distant hills.

Children in particular will enjoy
the frog and beetle markers that
set out a series of short, circular
walks through the young oak
woodland.

Orchids and butterflies bring
colour to the glades. Beneath
birch, hazel, holly and bracken
look for bilberries in the autumn.

As well as supporting a large
population of dormice, the wood
is festooned with lichens, mosses
and ferns, adding a wonderful
atmospheric quality.

Today the open meadows, which
are managed by grazing, are home
to the rare heath lobelia.

Once known as Stanton Moor –
meaning 'stony place', the site is
littered with quartzite boulders. Its
new name commemorates the life
of Andrew Walker whose parents
donated the wood to Devon
Wildlife Trust in his memory.

Newton Wood
Newton Ferrers

Access Newton Wood from village of Newton Ferrers (parking spaces at end of road near yacht club). Walk along public footpath which follows private lane (Court Wood) to wood entrance. (SX545488), 17ha (42acres), AONB
Woodland Trust

Popular with nearby communities, Newton Wood is semi-natural ancient woodland, and forms part of Yealm Woods.

Set in the South Devon Area of Outstanding Natural Beauty, Newton lies on the slopes of the River Yealm valley and is dominated by oak coppice. Some sections also feature mature high forest beech and sweet chestnut.

Look for the twisted shapes created by a clump of old Monterey pines. From here you will be rewarded with a fine view across the river, at the spot where the main river meets the creek on its northern boundary. The open ground below is a popular picnic site.

Amid the oak coppice, bluebells add a wonderful splash of colour each spring.

Across the river, your eye alights on another Woodland Trust wood called Hollacombe Quarry. From here it looks deceptively close but is in fact a drive away, and accessed from the village of Wembury.

Newton Wood

MAP 3

Tetbury

Cricklade

Wantage

Yate

Malmesbury

Red Lodge

Ravensroost Wood

Swindon

Chippenham

Calne

Clouts Wood

Marlborough

Hungerford

Bath

Melksham

Devizes

West Woods

Savernake Forest

Trowbridge

Green Lane Wood

Pewsey

North Wessex Downs

Radstock

Westbury

Ludgershall

Frome

Warminster

Andover

acon Hill Wood

Witham Park Woods

Amesbury

ton let

Stourhead Estate

Stockbridge

gswood arren

Mere

Wilton

Salisbury

Wincanton

Shaftesbury

Garston Wood

Blackmoor Copse

Fifehead Wood

Duncliffe Wood

Romsey

way Woods rbourne

Cranbourne Chase & West Wiltshire Downs

Tinneys Firs

Southampton

3030

Fordingbridge

ddleswood

Ashley Wood

Moors Valley Forest

Hythe

Blandford Forum

Kingston Lacy

Ringwood

New Forest

outh Hill lantation

Wimborne Minster

letown

Bournemouth

Christchurch

Wareham Forest

Poole

Isle of Wight

r Thorncombe Wood

Wool

Wareham

Isle of Purbeck

Swanage

91

MAP 3

Ravensroost Wood
Malmesbury

Take the B4696 Ashton Keynes road north from Wooton Bassett. After 3.2km (2 miles) take second left to Minety. Go straight on when the main road turns sharp right. Straight over next crossroads and car park on right.
(SU024877), 39ha (96acres), SSSI
Wiltshire Wildlife Trust

Spectacular displays of flowers such as bluebells, violets and primrose make this a wonderful venue for a spring visit.

At dawn on May mornings you can hear willow warblers, blackcap, chiffchaff and garden warblers, while winter sees nuthatches, tits and treecreepers moving noisily around.

Once part of the 40-square-mile Royal Hunting Forest of Braydon, Ravensroost is the largest remnant of ancient semi-natural woodland in the Braydon Forest. Parts of the site are still coppiced on a short-term and long-term rotation to provide stakes for hedgelaying as well as other timber products.

Today it is dominated by oak with a hazel understorey but includes the less common small-leaved lime and wild service tree which provide a superb display of autumn colour.

There is ample access, including a byway, bridleway and woodland rides. On their edges, look out for common spotted, early purple and great butterfly orchids. July and August are peak times to spot species such as silver-washed fritillary, white admiral, gatekeeper and peacock butterflies.

Red Lodge
Malmesbury

Located on B4696 south of village of Ashton Keynes a short distance after crossing the railway line whilst heading south, the wood is on the left.
(SU054888), 100ha (247acres)
Forestry Commission

Lush and lovely, this beautiful oak and hazel wood was once part of Braydon Forest, along with nearby Webb's Wood, Somerford Common and Ravensroost (see previous entry).

It can take a little determination to reach the wood, which is set next to a busy road and has no formal parking. You can park at nearby Somerford Common and

Webb's Wood and find your way via public footpaths – with a little help from an Ordnance Survey map.

The reward is the chance to savour a lush-feeling wood with a colourful ground cover of wildflowers including spurge laurel, bluebells, tansy, sedges, woodrush and mosses.

A delightful pond can be found at the north end of the site, which stands on level ground.

A series of rides and tracks crisscross the wood. However, there are no waymarkers so navigation is more of a challenge.

Clouts Wood
Wroughton

Follow A4361 out of Wroughton towards Avebury. Near top of hill park in lay-by on right.
(SU137794)
13ha (32acres), AONB, SSSI
Wiltshire Wildlife Trust

Spring is the best time to visit this small oak and ash woodland, when it is awash with bluebells.

Having parked in the lay-by near the top of the hill on the A4361 Avebury road out of Wroughton, walk back towards Wroughton, ignoring the first stile and joining a public footpath through the kissing gate, just past the 30mph sign. After a further stile you can follow the path down the hill, cross another stile and over footbridge to the entrance.

Your efforts will be rewarded with a mix of woods and sunny glades with a ground cover of elegant Bath asparagus, wood vech and nettle-leaved bellflower. Look for woodpeckers and tree creepers active above.

There is a series of trails through the wood, which lies on a slope. Wear wellies or boots as it is pretty muddy in places.

MAP 3

West Woods
Marlborough

Take A346 through Marlborough, then A345 towards Amesbury. Just after left turn to Clench Common, turn right to Morton and follow lane. Woods on left. Keep going until you see a gravel track and sign for wood on left. Follow forest track into wood, where car park is located.

(SU163667), 393ha (971acres)

Forestry Commission

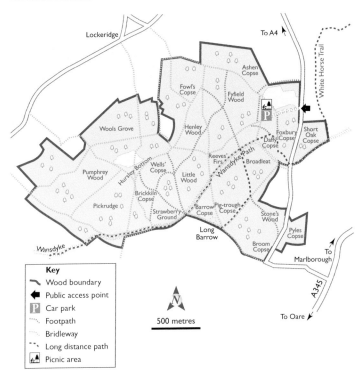

Key

⌒ Wood boundary
◀ Public access point
🅿 Car park
····· Footpath
····· Bridleway
- - - Long distance path
🏕 Picnic area

500 metres

Renowned for its spring sheets of bluebells, this 1930s beech plantation is a delightful surprise.

Despite this being a plantation, because beech dominates, a fair amount of light is able to filter through to the ground, eliminating the oppressiveness and monotony of some. The overall impression is of being in a painting of beeches – a place to get lost in time and space.

The well-maintained forest road acts as a main route for this well-cared-for forest with lots of paths and bridleways, all of which are well used by visitors.

Ash is regenerating on the edges of the forest tracks, giving a feeling of new life, compounded by the constant accompaniment of birdsong.

Dotted among the beech trees are holly, sycamore, ash and coppiced hazel, and this continues as far as the eye can see.

Its popularity is immediately obvious from the well-trodden state of its multiple bridleways.

Dogs are welcome but owners are asked to ensure they are kept on leads until well away from the car park as sheep are present in surrounding fields.

Bluebells adding their spring colour

MAP 3

Savernake Forest

Savernake Forest
Marlborough

From Marlborough, off the A346 towards Burbage. Postern Hill picnic site signposted off this road. (SU198679), 1000ha (2472acres)

Savernake Estate managed by Forestry Commission

Reputed to be the best ancient beech tree site in Europe, the royal hunting forest of Savernake boasts no fewer than 6,000 ancient trees.

This vast and hugely popular site is also well known for the old Roman road and the renowned 'Grand Avenue', though the latter can be frustratingly difficult to locate. However, with thousands of veteran trees, some great leisure opportunities and ample access, there is plenty to discover.

Sections of the forest are a mixture of deciduous and coniferous trees which offer a safe and relaxing atmosphere for children to play in.

Owned by the Earl of Cardigan it is leased by the Forestry Commission, which maintains a network of tracks and paths. However, don't expect waymarkers and signs. A tour by bicycle is a good way to explore a forest of this size.

Green Lane Wood
Trowbridge

Entrance to wood is on the A350 just south of Steeple Ashton traffic lights. Car park on west side of road. This is a fast road and the entrance is hidden – take care. (ST886577), 39ha (96acres)
Wiltshire Wildlife Trust

This lovely, small ancient woodland has much to interest both naturalists and historians alike.

Its northern boundary is marked by a medieval wood bank and ditch, bounded to the north by a wildflower-rich meadow. Elsewhere are signs the wood was once divided into four areas for coppicing.

Evidence suggests Green Lane Wood may pre-date the Domesday Book and the wide variety of species it supports – such as Solomon's seal and stinking iris – bear testimony to its age.

Traditional management methods are being used to attract rare butterflies such as the Duke of Burgundy and silver-washed fritillary.

The sunny southern side of the wood, where coppicing has opened up the canopy, is great for watching birds including nuthatches, tree creepers and great spotted and green woodpeckers.

A network of easy-to-walk rides and footpaths provides a springboard for exploration of the site, which boasts many oaks – perhaps once grown for a nearby 18th-century tannery.

MAP 3

Kingston Lacy
Wimborne

From B3082, 3km (2 miles) west of Wimborne, turn onto drive leading to the property and public car park 500m. Woodland walk accessed via reception.

(ST980019), 202ha (500acres) (whole estate 8500 acres), SSSI

National Trust

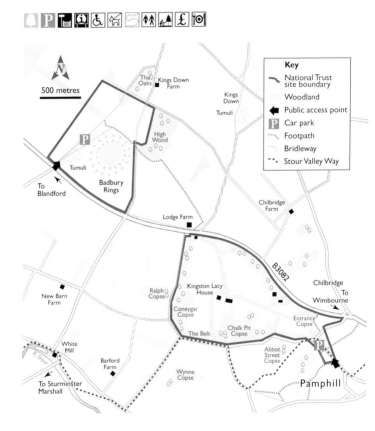

A famous, much-painted and photographed beech avenue lining the approach to the estate sets the tone for a visit to Kingston Lacy from the west – a grand landscape.

This massive, 8,500 acre estate, with sprawling woodland and parkland trees, has some delightful walks.

It's such an enormous landscape that it's best to give yourself a day to walk around, navigating from wood to hamlet to Badbury Rings with the help of a leaflet.

The estate is packed with contrast – the chalk land around Badbury Rings has large, rectangular fields, but beyond Kingston Lacy House and towards Wimborne, the character changes to a more intimate, older landscape with copses, woods and scattered hamlets linked by winding tracks.

One woodland – 'The Oaks' – boasts 12 pollarded veteran oaks dating back 500–600 years. Visitors are restricted to walking around the perimeter here, to help conserve this hugely important habitat.

From the western side of The Oaks, you gaze across the vast Dorset landscape, including 100 Acre Wood, a distant hazel coppice and once a wartime ammunition site.

Another feature is The Limes, a horseshoe-shaped series of common lime dating back to 1830. Elsewhere there is the chance to admire cedar rows.

Abbots Street Copse, at the Pampshill end of the estate, is a real crowd-puller in spring, when it is covered in sheets of bluebells.

Another big draw is the herd of handsome red Devon cows, which can be seen grazing beneath veteran parkland trees.

Kingston Lacy

MAP 3

Tinneys Firs
Salisbury

8km (5 miles) south of Salisbury
on A338, turn left signed
Downton. After approx 3km
(2 miles), just through Woodfalls,
turn left into Whiteshoot
Hill towards Lover. Car park 400m
(0.25 mile) on left.
(SU202200), 24ha (59acres)
Woodland Trust

Tinney's Firs nestles between the
rolling chalk hills of the West
Wiltshire Downs and the ancient
New Forest.

The wood is undulating and
features a host of small streams and
ditches. While this mature
woodland is dominated by oak, it
includes a wide variety of species
from beech and birch to Scots
pine, larch and yew.

The 'Firs' in its name refers to a
group of large Douglas fir which
grows around a house near the
centre of the wood.

A number of unusual ponds, an
old brick kiln and a well on the
northwest boundary, indicate the
wood's underlying landscape of
sand and clay.

Moors Valley Forest
Ringwood

Leave the A31 at Ashley Heath
roundabout and underpass taking
the Horton road in the direction
of Three Legged Cross. The
entrance to Moors Valley
approx.1.5km (1 mile) on right.
Follow brown tourist signs from
roundabout.
(SU107056)
303ha (750acres)
Forestry Commission

This vast conifer plantation is a
great recreational destination.

Choose from cycle hire, narrow
gauge steam railway, high ropes,
shop, visitor centre, golf, pitch and
putt, three lakes and a series of
small woods – this is a wonderful
place for a family day out.

Trails are very accessible and
leaflets help you to explore the site
which, while huge, is easy enough
to navigate. Cycle trails and walks
are well graded and very popular
with cyclists and families with
young children.

Venture into the forest to enjoy a
play trail complete with wooden
structures and tree-top trail.

Ashley Wood

Ashley Wood
Blandford Forum

Located next to golf course on B3082 just north of Tarrant Keyneston, southeast of Blandford Forum. (ST928048)

12ha (30acres)

Dorset Wildlife Trust

Seasonal colours of bluebells, wood anemone, violet, primrose and wild strawberry add to the attractions of this pleasant little oak and ash woodland.

Set in pretty Dorset countryside, there is plenty to take the visitor's mind off the sounds of the nearby road.

Crisscrossed with rides on good level ground, the site features scattered mature oaks and regenerating ash.

Look for hazel coppice where the new growth of long, straight stems is being used to create roughly woven fences around other hazel to protect the new growth from deer.

The larger Kingston Lacy estate (see page 98) is not far away and combining a visit to the two sites makes for a varied day out.

MAP 3

Piddleswood
Sturminster Marshall

From A357 Blandford to
Sherborne road, after Shillingstone
heading westwards, take a left after
the cemetery on left, at a
public house. Go up hill through
Broadwood, and fork left at
Copse Hill. 300 metres on left is
car park. (ST801135)
71ha (175acres), SSSI
Mr A Pitt-Rivers

Piddleswood appears not that
interesting at first but the further
you delve into its depths, the more
its varied story unfolds.

It's a little like a maze, full of
different woodland habitats and
the shrub layer is dense in places,
all adding to the wood's complex
personality.

The site actually comprises
several small and contrasting
woods including a 27-hectare
Wildlife Trust reserve that's
actively managed as a hazel
coppice with tall oaks rising
above.

Wild service tree, sweet chestnut
and cherry are among the
numerous species present here. In
spring and summer, blankets of
bluebells, wood anemones,
moschatel and early purple orchid
appear below.

The wood is home to a vast
array of insects and birds,
including 23 butterfly species,
green and great spotted
woodpecker and the increasingly
scarce dormouse which makes its
nest among the dense shrubby
hazel layer.

Monmouth Hill/ Ruins Plantation
Milton Abbas

From the A354 Blandford Forum
to Dorchester road, follow signs to
Milton Abbas. From village, take
minor road past church, at end of
the lake, up the hill. Monmouth hill
is on right at top of hill. Parking by
wood entrance.
(ST797015), 34ha (84acres),
AONB, SSSI

Forestry Commission

Set amid stunning countryside, the
beech plantation of Monmouth
Hill is worth a visit to appreciate
the part it plays in a landscape
which includes several other
woodlands.

The plantation is a designated
site of special scientific interest set

Monmouth Hill

within the Purbeck Area of Outstanding Natural Beauty.

It hugs the hillside overlooking the school in the village of Milton Abbas. Around it are wide, sweeping open fields, large wooded valleys, thatched cottages and other beautiful buildings.

Monmouth Hill runs into Ruins Plantation as well as a coppice and a dew pond that is managed by the school. There is also a medieval agricultural terrace.

The plantation itself is a mix of beech and conifers, currently being thinned to encourage deciduous species.

It's possible to devise a circular walk through the plantation but this is perhaps best avoided in winter when the tracks can get badly churned up by horses.

MAP 3

Wareham Forest
Wareham

From the A351 at Wareham,
heading towards the train station,
take minor road northwest
towards Cold Harbour and
Wareham Forest. The Sika Trail car
park is on right.
(SY905893), 1542ha (3811acres)
Forestry Commission

This vast forest of conifers,
interspersed with heathland exudes
a sense of wildness, peace and space.

The greens of the conifers
against the browns and purple of
the heath and the rust and yellow
of the gorse create a patchwork of
wonderful colours whatever the
time of year.

While popular, the site has a
feeling of a vast and open space.
Within the forest in summer you
can hear buzzards and green
woodpeckers or nightjars on the
heath and smell the fresh aroma of
pine, heather and gorse.

A hike up to the Iron Age hill
fort is worth the effort, for here
you get a real feel for the
heathland of Thomas Hardy's day
though the forest is a more recent
addition.

The vast network of well-
maintained tracks stretches for
miles and work is under way on a
cycle trail from Wareham Station
through the forest.

Thorncombe Wood
Dorchester

From A35 east of Dorchester take
minor road at roundabout signed
Higher Bockhampton, then first
left, following signs to Hardy's
Cottage. Car park for woods near
cottage.
(SY725921), 26ha (64acres)
Dorset County Council

This is a 'not to be missed'
woodland in the heart of Thomas
Hardy country, which offers lots of
variety and atmosphere.

An ancient semi-natural site of
oak, sweet chestnut and beech, it's
dotted with hazel coppice and
conifers and merges naturally into
its neighbour, Puddletown Forest.

The dormouse, song thrush,
marsh tit and lesser spotted
woodpecker have made
Thorncombe their home. There is
an impressive list of butterflies
such as orange tip, common blue,
small tortoiseshell, brimstone,
green-veined white, red admiral

and silver-studded blue.

An ancient Roman road wends its way through the wood while a network of rides rambles up and down. Conifers include Scots pine, Douglas fir, Monterey pine and coast redwood. Look out too for some wonderful ancient beeches and, in spring, an abundance of bluebells, violets and wood anemones.

There is also a heath featuring three species of heather.

Thorncombe Wood

Hooke Park
Beaminster

Take A356 Crewkerne to Dorchester road. Turn right into B3163, signed Beaminster. Take first left and follow round until wood is on right. There is a large lay-by for parking.
(ST525003), 141ha (350acres)
Architectural Association Inc

An absence of welcoming signals should not deter the visitor from venturing into Hooke Park. This large commercial woodland is well worth a visit.

A sole entrance gate with warnings to keep to roads and public paths and keep dogs on a lead greet the visitor, but carry on undeterred and there is a lot to explore.

Full of birdsong and other wildlife – including owls and deer – the wood has an open feel to it with lots of light filtering through.

It's a varied wood, with a mix of conifers and broadleaves including some wonderful beech, Sitka spruce and oaks.

The forest tracks are dotted with wide, open glades. Particularly interesting landmarks along a circular path are the Architectural Association School of Architecture buildings. Designed by teams dedicated to pushing the boundaries of building with wood, Westminster Lodge features a grass roof and the extensive use of unmilled, untreated timber.

MAP 3

Axmouth to Lyme Regis Undercliffs
Seaton and Lyme Regis

Access to the site is provided along the South West Coast Path. Use either the upper or lower car park in Lyme Regis or at Seaton, just before entering on the B3172, park in lay-by on left just before golf club. Lyme Regis access point (SY332916). Seaton access point (SY264903).
331ha (818acres), AONB, SSSI
English Nature

The undercliff is the area between the sea cliff and the inland cliff. This is a walk on the wild side – a unique 'green' world that has escaped man's influence.

Every surface in this reserve seems covered in ivy and moss and even in late autumn, the wood is very green and offers shelter from the elements.

A succession of landslides has created internationally important habitats, including open ground, grassland, wetland and scrub.

For the visitor the result is fantastic. The cliff tops at the start of the walk from Seaton offers great views of Seaton Bay.

Ash and sycamore dominate but look out too for holly, hazel, and more unusually, holme oak and western red cedar. There is also lots of varied ground vegetation.

The ground – a mix of ridges and hollows, deep gullies and areas of large, moss and ivy-clad boulders – makes walking arduous so sturdy boots – and fitness – are recommended.

Kings Wood
Winscombe

Turn off A38 between Axbridge and Winscombe 1.5km (1 mile) north of Axbridge into Winscombe Road. Car park on left.
(ST422561), 15ha (38acres), SSSI
National Trust

A delightful ancient woodland site adorning the eastern slopes of Winscome Hill on the southern side of the Mendip.

Small-leaved lime pollards dating back 400 years are among the main species here, along with some large and mature ash, oak, wild cherry and field maple. Spring-flowering wild garlic and wood anemone create a creamy white carpet beneath.

This is an easy-to-walk and delightful-to-discover site with added interest in the shape of a medieval boundary bank and ditch that can still be seen inside the wood. In fact, many of the larger lime pollards grow on top of the bank.

Because the old coppice stools are well spaced, plenty of light dapples the woodland floor. A short circular walk leads walkers along well-defined paths through different sections of the site.

Long Wood
Cheddar

North of B3135 through Cheddar Gorge. Park at Black Rock Gate car park and walk north along West Mendip Way to wood. (ST482545)
19ha (47acres), AONB, SSSI
Somerset Wildlife Trust

The history of Long Wood is almost as deep as the dramatic Cheddar Gorge lying immediately south.

Spring is one of the best times to visit this spectacular valley when the woodland floor is clothed in bluebells, wild garlic and dog's mercury, dotted with wood anemone, primrose and yellow archangel.

A semi-natural ancient wood, it was once owned by the medieval monks of the Carthusian Priory at Witham who managed it by coppicing.

More recently in the 1950s, it was felled and replanted with beech and conifers, a policy now reversed to encourage ash and hazel regeneration.

There is much here to delight – even the approach from Black Rock car park, beneath vertical limestone cliffs and across close-topped turf – which is perfect for picnics.

In the damp, shady valley mosses, hart's tongue fern and opposite-leaved golden saxifrage thrive. A stream running through the northern part of the reserve disappears underground into Long Wood Swallet cave.

Dogs are welcome but must be kept on a lead.

MAP 3

Ebbor Gorge
Wells

From A371 turn at Easton towards Wookey Hole. After 1.5km (1 mile) turn left up narrow lane towards Priddy. Car park on right after a short drive.
(ST525485), 41ha (101acres), SSSI
English Nature

A visit to Ebbor Gorge is quickly rewarded with some stunning views across the Levels from various vantage points, including the car park and cliff top.

The deep limestone gorge, created by the collapse of caves on the Mendip's southern scarp, is now wooded with ash, oak and

Ebbor Gorge

hazel coppice. It is particularly colourful in spring, thanks to carpets of bluebells, wood anemone, violets and yellow archangel.

A series of waymarked trails with good access makes this wooded gorge a place that anyone can enjoy. Routes range from a short trail, suitable for wheelchairs and buggies, to longer and more challenging circuits.

One route leads into the valley through coppice woodland and small meadows. Good strong footwear is recommended for the longest and most strenuous trail – a scramble through the gorge between towering limestone cliffs.

Wherever you explore, there are delightful views to reward you.

Tor Hill
Wells

Tor Hill is located alongside B3159 Wells to Dulcote Road or 500m walk from Wells Cathedral (ST554458), 6ha (15acres)
National Trust

Small can be beautiful – and full of interest, as Tor Hill proves. Even better – it's just five minutes' walk from the heart of Wells.

Lying on the western end of a ridge, the site features two strips of woodland separated by an area of open grassland on the flat hilltop.

The woodland along the northern scarp, through which most access paths run, is a great place to explore. The woodland floor is undulating, with rocky limestone outcrops and small cliffs.

Just inside the entrance there is a mix of native and ornamental species including large holm oak, Scots pine, cedar, oak, beech, ash and yew.

Where the wood becomes more semi-natural, ivy and hart's tongue fern make way for dog's mercury and other characteristic woodland flora.

A network of occasionally steep paths gives access to the meadow from where you can admire views of Wells Cathedral and the Mendip.

MAP 3

Beacon Hill Wood
Shepton Mallet

North of Shepton Mallet on A37 take third right into Old Frome Road (just before A367 turning to Bath). Wood 800m (0.5 mile) on right with space for 3 to 4 cars at entrance. (ST639459)

17ha (42acres)

Woodland Trust

Steep climbs, stunning scenery… and secret agents all form part of the unusual mix that makes Beacon Hill Wood a fascinating place to visit and popular with locals.

A prominent landscape feature, visible for miles, a clump of large old beech trees at the centre form a distinctive crown on the ridge.

The wood is archaeologically important with features dating back to Neolithic, Bronze Age and Roman times.

Bronze Age barrows (burial mounds), old quarry pits and various standing stones are just some of the features to look for. The great Roman road known as the Fosse Way crosses through the wood although its exact route is uncertain.

More recently the Auxiliary Unit, one of the most secret services of World War Two had a base here, operating out of an underground bunker.

Today's visitors can explore its springs, gullies and ridges and ponds, rides and glades. In spring, sections are carpeted with bluebells.

Beacon Hill Wood

Witham Park Woods
Maiden Bradley – Frome

From A350 1.5km (1 mile) south of junction with A36 at Crockerton, turn off main road and follow signs to Maiden Bradley. Straight ahead at crossroads in Maiden Bradley, follow road to T junction beside woods. Turn right and then left into lane leading to Witham Park Farm. Car park on right. (ST771392), 190ha (470acres)
Duke of Somerset

Witham Park Woods are a commercial plantation – but managed to provide the best for wildlife, the landscape and for the visitors who use the site for recreation.

The result is a mixture of commerce, conservation and aesthetics that provides a home for woodland birds and deer and includes some good views across the Somerset countryside. Its two waymarked routes could be combined to create a longer walk.

Most of the site is high forest with plantations of Douglas fir, larch, western hemlock, Norway spruce, Scots pine and western red cedar. Many of the stands are nearing maturity and careful thinning has created attractive open areas with views through the forest, and an understorey of younger trees and shrubs.

Other sections have deciduous trees such as birch, rowan, alder, hazel and oak, some planted for conservation and landscape reasons.

Adjacent is Marston Wood, which rises steeply to the east to a high area of beech with an impressive show of bluebells.

MAP 3

Stourhead Estate

Mere

Signposted from A303 and B3092. King Alfred's Tower is 5.5km (3.5 miles) by road from Stourhead House. (ST748354)

123ha (304acres) AONB

National Trust

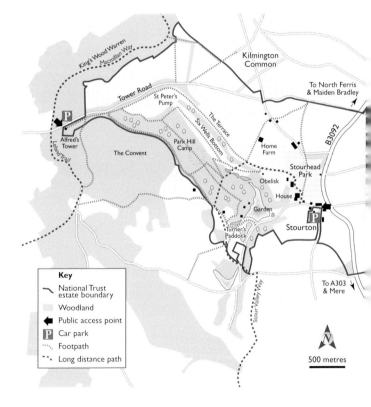

Stourhead Estate

You get double the choice on a visit to Stourhead Estate, with two contrasting woodland experiences up for grabs.

The first allows you to explore large expanses of coniferous woodlands and mixed woodland at no cost; the second allows you – for the price of admission – to explore the fine 18th-century landscape gardens.

If you opt for the former, start out from King Alfred's tower, three-and-a-half miles from the main estate entrance. The energetic can attempt the tower stairs before heading out into vast expanses of majestic coniferous forests on the estate and nearby Stourhead Western.

The tracks are muddy and rough and the walk enclosed by seemingly miles of conifers but the occasional glimpse of the landscape is truly beautiful. There are also impressively large deciduous trees to enjoy.

In the garden you have the opportunity to walk amongst a mix of exotic coniferous and deciduous trees. The extensive list of wildlife recorded here includes many species of birds, wood wasps, wood ants, 30 butterfly species – including white admiral and silver-washed fritillary – along with long-eared owls, nightingales and buzzards.

Henry Hoare ll began the landscape garden at Stourhead in 1744, creating a lake around which he planted many tree species typical to the area. The result was a vista reminiscent of 18th-century landscape paintings. There are also small groups of grand conifers in contrasting hues, some of which seem to hug the ancient oaks.

Notable features of the site include amazing veteran sweet chestnut trees and exquisite views of the Pantheon, framed by the hanging branches of beeches, dense laurel, rocky knolls and water cascades. The site is a melee of colour and texture, with the feeling of lush meadows and woodland tumbling down to meet the lakeside.

MAP 3

Stourhead (Western) Estate Woodlands
Mere

Follow B3092 north from Mere, towards Frome; take third left signed towards Alfred's Tower, then first left down Tower Road. Car park on right after 1.5km (1 mile). (ST748353), 651ha (1609acres), AONB

Nick Hoare, Stourhead (Western) Estate

This mixed woodland is set in a changing landscape, from deep sheltered combes to 100m-high plateaux, ensuring the visitor is always kept intrigued.

The site is being managed to give continuous cover, with much emphasis on regeneration, in addition to the ecological and recreational benefits of the area.

Among the conifers are some particularly magnificent specimens, especially Douglas fir. Visitors can explore the site via an extensive forest-track network but since this is an active site, it is important to stick with the tracks and to heed any warning signs.

Kingswood Warren
Mere

As above. (ST748353) 133ha (330acres), AONB

Mr H C Hoare

A dynamic wood of many contrasts, Kingswood Warren, part of an extensive wooded escarpment, lies north of the main (Stourhead Western) estate.

Much of the site's upper scarp features mature larch, with a strip of mixed broadleaves running along the top. The lower slopes are dominated by young conifers, most planted in the 1980s.

The Hoare family, who own and manage the site, aim eventually to bring broadleaves lower down the slope, boosting the broadleaf-conifer mix.

There is a good circular route, via a forest track, which takes in all the main features of the site. This can be taken up by entering the site north of the car park, through an area of woodland known as Jack's Castle.

Because this is a working site, visitors are asked to stick to the forest tracks and heed any warning signs.

Holway Woods
Sherborne

Take the B3145 from Sherborne
towards Charlton Hawthorne,
turning west at Poyntington
Crossroads then straight over the
next junction to Holway.
(ST632205), 16ha (40acres)
Dorset Wildlife Trust

Small, unassuming and rather
lovely, Holway Wood has much to
recommend it to visitors – if they
are fit and well shod.

There are few indications that
this site, which sits on a steep
slope, is open to the public and a
level of fitness is needed to tackle
its short, occasionally slippery
path. However, those who do
discover a richly varied, natural
woodland with impressive rural
views.

The lower slopes are populated
mainly with hazel coppice, some of
it large and impressive. There are
also ash, field maple, and sycamore
and big old oaks. Higher up, sweet
chestnut and oak have been
planted but it looks as though
squirrels have frequently got there
first. There is a wealth of ground
flora and some wonderful ferns.

From the top are fantastic
countryside views and locals say,
on a clear day, you can see as far as
Glastonbury Tor and the
Quantock Hills.

MAP 3

Duncliffe Wood
Shaftesbury

From Shaftesbury town centre follow A30 west for 6.5km (4 miles). At Kings Arms turn left for Stour Row. After 1km (0.75 mile) park in narrow layby and follow bridleway into wood. (ST826222), 87ha (215acres)

Woodland Trust

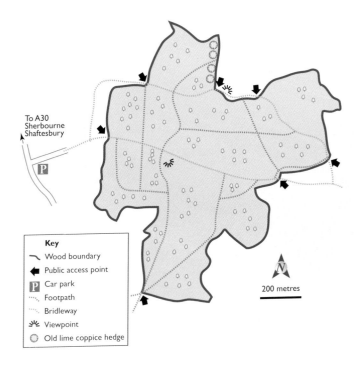

To A30
Sherbourne
Shaftesbury

Key
- ⌒ Wood boundary
- ◀ Public access point
- 🅿 Car park
- ⋯ Footpath
- ⋯ Bridleway
- ⚜ Viewpoint
- ◎ Old lime coppice hedge

N

200 metres

Duncliffe Wood

Prominent on the summits of Duncliffe Hill, just west of Shaftesbury, and rising out of Blackmoor Vale, this large ancient woodland site can be spotted from miles around.

A designated site of nature conservation interest, it has a rich mix of woodland species, including what are reported to be the oldest living things in Dorset – a scattering of coppice stools of small-leaved limes.

Once an oak, ash and hazel woodland, the site was traditionally coppiced but was felled and replanted in the 1950s and 60s with a mix of Norway spruce, oak, larch and beech.

In recent years, however, there has been a move away from beech and the site is managed in a way that encourages a broader mix of native broadleaves.

Here you will find an array of Dorset 'notable' species include moschatel, yellow archangel, wood speedwell and early purple orchid.

The wood is a reservoir of wildlife with a rich butterfly mix including silver-washed fritillary, white admiral and purple hairstreak. Other resident wildlife includes roe deer, badgers, tawny owls, bats and an array of birds such as buzzards, woodpeckers and treecreepers.

Surrounding the woodland, the landscape is characterised by sweeping valleys and rounded hills with woodland dominating the scarp faces. However, pasture predominates in the area and the woods are almost enveloped by improved grassland, adding to the dramatic impact of the site on the local scene.

MAP 3

Fifehead Wood
Fifehead Magdalen

Turn off A30 west of Shaftesbury,
signed Fifehead Magdalen. After
800m (0.5 mile) park in layby
opposite wood entrance.
(ST773215), 20ha (49acres)

Woodland Trust

A haven in an otherwise sparsely
wooded landscape, Fifehead Wood
is a rich wildlife resource known
for its important moth and
butterfly populations – this is the
only known place in Dorset to find
the light orange underwing moth.

Records show no fewer than 24
different butterfly species, including
purple hairstreak and white admiral
and its breeding-bird population
includes herons, great spotted
woodpeckers and tree creepers.

Lying next to the village of
Fifehead Magdalen, this attractive
mixed-broadleaf site sits in the
heart of the Blackmoor Vale, on the
edge of the Stour Valley and is a
popular walking spot for local
villagers.

Believed to date back to a
medieval park, Fifehead Wood has
been designated a site of nature
conservation interest. In spring the
pathways are edged with bluebells,
early purple orchid, wood
anemone, moschatel and yellow
pimpernel.

Fifehead Wood

Garston Wood
Sixpenny Handley

From the A354 Salisbury to
Blandford road turn to the village
of Sixpenny Handley on the
B3031, turning right onto the
Broad Chalke road. The wood is
on the left, with the car park at the
northernmost end of the wood.
(SU004194)
34ha (84acres), AONB, SSSI
RSPB

The ancient art of coppicing
helped shape this wonderful
woodland – as well as playing an
important part in the local
economy.

Among 20 different species of
trees are tall oak and ash, hazel and
maple coppice.

Garston teems with life – home
to hares, squirrels, deer, dormice
and badgers, birdlife galore from
turtle doves, blackcaps, garden
warblers, willow warblers and bull
finch to tits, gold crests,
treecreepers, woodcock, fieldfares
and redwings.

There is also an abundance of
butterflies. You might glimpse a
grizzled skipper, silver-washed
fritillary, white admiral and purple
hairstreak or any one of 26 other
species found here.

And the woods look and smell
stunning in spring and summer
with wild garlic, bluebells,
primroses, violets and bird's nest
orchid growing alongside the good
network of rides and paths.

MAP 3

Blackmoor Copse
Salisbury

9.5km (6 miles) east of Salisbury,
the wood is on minor road
between Winterslows and East
Grimstead. Main entrance at
junction of Ben Lane and the road
to East Grimstead. (SU234288).
36ha (89acres)

Wiltshire Wildlife Trust

Famed for its dormice and huge
array of butterflies – 30 of the 55
species in Britain – this is a site of
delights and intrigue.

They take many forms: spring
carpets of woodland flowers such
as primroses, bluebells and wood
anemones or summer hordes of
sun-loving butterflies, like the
silver-washed fritillary. Lucky
visitors might spot a shy roe deer
hiding in the undergrowth.

The intrigue comes from the
unknown origins of a magnificent
row of yews and the significance
of the curiously named King
Charles' Pond.

The woods are being managed
to create the best conditions for
rare butterfly species by allowing
light into the dense woodland.

As there are few real landmarks
in the wood it would be fairly
easy to become disorientated, but
this is a small site so there's little
risk of getting lost.

WOODLAND
TRUST

Trees and forests are crucial to life on our planet. They generate oxygen, play host to a spectacular variety of wildlife and provide us with raw materials and shelter. They offer us tranquillity, inspire us and refresh our souls.

Founded in 1972, the Woodland Trust is now the UK's leading woodland conservation charity. By acquiring sites and campaigning for woodland it aims to conserve, restore and re-establish native woodland to its former glory. The Trust now owns and cares for over 1,100 woods throughout the UK.

The Woodland Trust wants to see:
no further loss of ancient woodland
the variety of woodland wildlife restored and improved
an increase in new native woodland
an increase in people's understanding and enjoyment of woodland

The Woodland Trust has 150,000 members who share this vision. For every new member, the Trust can care for approximately half an acre of native woodland. For details of how to join the Woodland Trust please either ring FREEPHONE 0800 026 9650 or visit the website at www.woodland-trust.org.uk.

If you have enjoyed the woods in this book please consider leaving a legacy to the Woodland Trust. Legacies of all sizes play an invaluable role in helping the Trust to create new woodland and secure precious ancient woodland threatened by development and destruction. For further information please either call 01476 581129 or visit our dedicated website at www.legacies.org.uk

Newton Wood

Further Information

Public transport

Each entry gives a brief description of location, nearest town and grid reference. Traveline provides impartial journey planning information about all public transport services either by ringing 0870 608 2608 (calls charged at national rates) or visit www.traveline.org.uk. For information about the Sustrans National Cycle Network either ring 0117 929 0888 or visit www.sustrans.org.uk

Useful contacts

Forestry Commission, 0845 367 3787, www.forestry.gov.uk
National Trust, 0870 458 4000, www.nationaltrust.org.uk
Wildlife Trusts, 0870 036 7711, www.wildlifetrusts.org
RSPB, 01767 680551, www.rspb.org.uk
Royal Forestry Society, 01442 822028, www.rfs.org.uk
National Community Forest Partnership, 01684 311880, www.communityforest.org.uk
Tree Council, 020 7407 9992, www.treecouncil.org.uk
Woodland Trust, 01476 581111, www.woodland-trust.org.uk
South West Forest, 01409 221896, www.southwestforest.org.uk

Recommend a Wood

You can play a part in helping us complete this series. We are inviting readers to nominate a wood or woods they think should be included. We are interested in any woodland with public access in England, Scotland, Wales and Northern Ireland.

To recommend a wood please photocopy this page and provide as much of the following information as possible:

About the wood

Name of wood: _____

Nearest town: _____

Approximate size: _____ ha/acres

Owner/manager: _____

A few words on why you think it should be included:

_____

_____

About you

Your name: _____

Your postal address: _____

_____

_____ Post code: _____

If you are a member of the Woodland Trust please provide your membership number.

Please send to: Exploring Woodland Guides, The Woodland Trust, Autumn Park, Dysart Road, Grantham, Lincolnshire NG31 6LL, by fax on 01476 590808 or e-mail woodlandguides@woodland-trust.org.uk

Thank you for your help

Other Guides in the Series

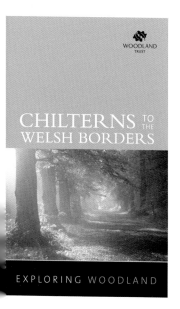

Chilterns to the Welsh Borders
Published April 2006

Coming soon

The South East of England

The Peak District
and Central England

Wales

If you would like to be notified when certain titles are due for
publication please either write to Exploring Woodland Guides,
The Woodland Trust, Autumn Park, Dysart Road, Grantham,
Lincolnshire NG31 6LL or e-mail woodlandguides@woodland-
trust.org.uk

Index

Legal & General is delighted to support the Woodland Trust's conservation programme across the UK.

As a leading UK company, Legal & General recognises the importance of maintaining and improving our environment for future generations. We actively demonstrate our commitment through good management and support of environmental initiatives and organisations, such as the Woodland Trust.

Information on how Legal & General manages its impact on the environment can be found at www.legalandgeneralgroup.com/csr.